The Beautiful Losses

Frederick Pollack

Better Than Starbucks
Publications

The Beautiful Losses

Copyright © 2023 by Frederick Pollack

All rights reserved. This book or any portion thereof may not be reproduced or used in any manner whatsoever without the express written permission of author and the publisher except for the use of brief quotations in a book review or scholarly journal.

First Printing: ISBN 978-1-7376219-5-9

Cover Image: "Cenote" by Phylis Geller

Better Than Starbucks Publications
P.O.Box 673, Mayo, FL 32066

And we walked above them, already far from the city shutting its gates behind us, knowing we would not return, since ahead of us lay space.

Marcel Brion

for Phylis

Table of Contents

Why Not	1
Robocall	2
Swivel	3
Total	4
Piety	5
Black Site	6
Still Thinking of Travel	7
The Thermos	8
Proof of Concept	10
Testament	11
Call	12
On Culture	13
Must Go On	14
Context	15
Sidekick	16
Excursion	17
Events of Today	18
The Central Committee	19
And So You Shall	20
HR	22
Mimesis	23
Entanglement	24
Old Mirror	25
Night in the Zone	26
You May Find Yourself	28
Role Model	30
The Cicerone	31
Colonel Bogey	32
Paintings of Texas Towns	33
When Names Drop	34
Gate of Horn	35
Gleam	36
Drive	38
Assignment	39
Enemies of the Paranoiac	40

Crasher	41
The Bells	42
Three "I" Poems	44
Ideal Glass	46
Geneva	47
Reform	48
Vieira da Silva	49
Meeting	50
Infrastructure	52
Late Valentine	56
Legacy	57
Déjeuner sur l'Herbe	58
Skull	59
Release	60
Erased	61
Among the Elders	62
Line from Eliot	64
Baron's Blues	65
The Toys	66
Incident	68
The Hutch	69
Alright	70
The Void	71
Between the Acts	72
Template	73
Locale	74
Old Trial	75
Vergangenheitsbewältigung	76
The Draw	77
The Perks	78
Firebird	79
The Coin	80
Solidarity	82
One Thing or Another	83
Darlin' you just sorta	84

The Prophet Drinks	85
Ballo in Maschera	86
Glyph	87
Namatianus	88
Something I Said	89
Friends	90
Echo	92
Vision in Georgetown	93
Low Orbit	94
Witsec	96
Empty Parable	97
The Towel	98
For the Centenary of H. S. Mauberley	99
Dig	100
No Problem	101
Group	102
Brood X	103
Figures in a Room	104
High End	105
Before They Dropped Salads	106
Sermon	108
Grasp	109
Line from Paul Engle	110
Cardinal or Oriole	111
Old Song	112
Late June	113
The Restaurant at the End of the Universe	114
The Beautiful Losses	115
Safe House	118
The Fortunate	120
View of San Francisco from the Hills	123

Acknowledgements

About the Author

Why Not

We'll have to keep the place
since no one has met our price, or can.
The wave will pass to the north and south;
the noise of people it lifts and chews
will be like that of quarrels
in distant cities or ethnicities.
Afterwards, creatures
deposited on our patch of beach
will spasm, crawl, or ooze
back to the sea. (Perhaps we'll go out
to help them!) When the sun
has been high for months, we'll raise
an umbrella; and fauns, bunnies,
strays will shelter on our happy lawn
beneath it, till rain returns
and, begging to stay, they leave.
Our fridge, the size of love,
will be a joy to open on ever-new
dishes or, if we choose
to cook, ingredients. We'll always
have news, since we are the news.
Shows about us. Games if we're bored.
Power.

Robocall

Fast snow like lint, like
Lucretian atoms, like mobilized
static, frosting the skylight.
Then, sounding first
like metal, rain
dissolving the ice. Day
extends. Throughout,
a view of unexcitedly
connected forces.
No calls. If there were,
they would be the breathing
of madmen, the hesitant,
the erroneous, the dead, or
the silence of machines,
cursed when you're sure they're gone.

Swivel

At last I turned it around
to face the window. Such wealth!
Paired neighbor trees, all trunk —
they were here before the neighborhood —
conversing, why not,
about conditions, their and human doom
as a function of entropy.
Middle-distance duplexes, a childhood
memory: not understanding
work and commutes, I thought
a darkened window meant someone was hiding.
Sky and clouds wishing
there were only one flag —
a bicolor, no irrelevance of blood —
everywhere beneath them.

It wasn't long before
I returned to the other view:
a corner of the room
above the black television,
faint transient bars of light, the walls one
of the innumerable shades
of beige one chooses.

Total

Spectacularly mangled, but not
in pain (the drip by now has become a flow),
except for the wish, so total it's spiritual,
for a drink. With the mind's remaining eye
he sees and pities
his car. He speaks, though without
needed amplification, expressing
love for several figures who appear,
unchanged by time, and without
remembered lawyers. Their looks
are love, but the mighty voice he hears
isn't theirs. Or the doc's (unless in some sense
it is): "It's no small feat
to have gone as far as fast as you.
It is speed alone that gives weight to things,
and you therefore are now considerable."

Piety

If you aren't watching when, days late,
the recycling truck arrives (it never
quite stops, and its crew must move
like figures in early films), you
may hear in hydraulic jacks,
descending maw, shaken bins, shouts
and brakes reassurance
that the faith of your grandparents' youth
still obtains. That there is a real world,
blast furnaces. That the ring which embraced
your beers will not end
in fish, nor the dust of cans
in you. That somewhere a building,
immaculate and huge, in its heart
a fire, several complex stellar fires,
stands. And the trucks and flatcars
feed those fires, which melt everything
(imagine the few, heroic workers!)
into ingots, some poisonous,
some almost gold. All waiting to be shipped
(for nothing, as you often pray, is lost)
to other factories, they sit
in mountainous piles, on squares whose pattern
strikes you as familiar . . . of course!
It's the Periodic Table.

Black Site

An unmarked plane is an inside joke;
it brings supplies, or a package.
The package is a man, but really a package.
Where it lands, desert, formerly picturesque
heath, is also funny and anomalous,
no longer marked on maps or of interest
to satellites. The package is brought
to a room without amenities,
whose absence represents both
your sacrifice and his unworthiness.
You begin by pointing this out.

Pain isn't the point; some philosophers
assert you don't feel another's.
Nor is it information
if it turns out he has none. The point, ultimately,
is procedure, as it must be for experienced
doctors. And privately to avoid
the sense of being too far away
from the world. Which you're not —
the canteen has the right food, the rec room
games, and any past
is an inferior sketch that needs erasure.

Still Thinking of Travel

That austere beauty
a monument to stupidity:
they cut down all the trees.
Then for centuries
they were owned, hungry,
tough, stunted, religious,
ill. Volcanoes and earthquakes,
two continental plates
rending a rockfield.

Roots like cobras
thread the voluptuous ruins. Only
fools and rude children
stop smiling. The Buddha
encourages some killing. Wear white
crisp short-sleeve
shirts to the demo. A certain
kind of hysterics
is reserved for soldiers.

But for the most part I
stay home. When fever comes,
a wet, cold – very cold –
washcloth descends
on my brow, and for
the never-expected
allover shaking
cold, one that is well-wrung
and warm,

my eyes shut tight throughout.

The Thermos

Our host wasn't what I'd expected —
all ego-twitch and flashing LEDs —
but a perfect imitation of grace.
We sat equidistant from the wing
with hip-hop for his younger guests
and the one where a string quartet
exhausted itself, hearing neither.
He talked about art — it was all on his walls —
and wine — he owned the patent.
Eventually the other cologned and perfumed
elites bowed off to
their suites. Still wakeful,
I said that with his permission I would take

a stroll. — Calm night, waning moon.
He had cornered the market on spring.
Among the trees and their tactful lanterns,
paired youngsters fresh from the dance
and some elders in search of exertion
lay on unobtrusive chaises
or grass. There was no need, I thought,
for statuary, had it been in style —
not with these classical, unsurpassable forms,
half-lit, half-shadowed, some partly draped,
sighing like wind. I wondered
if there were any other animals
in the forest — even a mosquito —

and made my way to the gazebo
half-visible beside a pond or sea.
There, my back to the revelers,
I sat on a fretwork chair. On the table
stood a thermos. A note seemed addressed to me,
though it only told whoever
sought rest here that this tea
had been placed late enough
it should still be hot. It was also,
said the note, delicious —
the rarest blend from our host's plantations —
and went on in this way so fulsomely
that, thirsty and chilled, I passed the offer by.

Proof of Concept

Knowing a poet is a curse,
worse if you're one. His readers,
insofar as they existed,
weren't. He was sick of their
attributing incidents and "feelings"
in his poems to "you," i.e., him.
Sometimes they even said they heard
his voice. He lost it, said Yes,
I saw that, I felt it,
one beautiful day last summer, during
the plague. It's all about me.
Don't go — you're me too.

Began to put the names of poets,
dead, famous, or neither in
his poems. Wished he had –
like William Corbett and Kenneth Irby —
poets as drinking buddies.
He did it so they would admire him
and he could fulfill
Auden's line: "he became his admirers."

Testament

Of myself I say only
I was not starved or beaten,
and leave it to those who were
to speak, so much more poignantly,
of their lives, and even,
if they can make anything of it,
mine. *He who has suffered you
to impose on him knows you,*
said Blake. He who has suffered you
knows you, but you know
the codes, the combination,
the right numbers to call,
and where the bodies are buried.

Of myself I say only
that as a child I suffered
the lack of a spirit animal.
There were cats, whose mastery
I recognized early,
and a dog that bit me.
Seagulls appeared in my twenties,
marginal scavengers
pressed into service as symbols of freedom,
hovering mornings and evenings
above a stone plaza.

Call

An office as tenuous
as fog. Someone unpaid
except in their own youth mans
the phone, the computer.
Never enough
money, time, ventilation, coffee,
understanding or patience,
though the latter is total.
Even the word "client" marks
a defeat somewhere
in deep time, a failure of
relationship.
Lawyers have clients, but law here
is the opponent in a perpetual
judo. And is
the one crying
or barely verbal on
the phone, who is bleeding
("from wherever"), evicted, hungry,
to be killed for "honor,"
guilty since birth, a client?
Doctors at least have patients,
but how to diagnose
one who calls without power
while the one who answers
has no power but answering?

I who don't belong here, tired
of Grand Hotel Abyss, wanted
to praise heroes,
and am immature enough
to imagine an armed, confident
man. But all I found,
all anyone can find
are mice in the granary of suffering,
and the advice of Lenin
that, finally, revolution
is an affair of clerks and accountants.

On Culture

On a ledge under a clerestory
window, playing sedately
with the light, a mask like a face
or a face like a mask. Pale
blue-green, features barely
incised in powdery
ceramic as if hidden
beneath the threshold of expression.
Despite himself, my guest is drawn to it.
"Often when I look at it," I say,
"I think of Cycladic sculptures —
those beings who hug themselves thin
as if preparing for some reason
to be fish or arrows — too snooty
for any organ but a nose.
I always wanted one of those,
but of course . . ." "Where's it from?" he growls.
"I've no idea," I lie.
"It could be very ancient."
"Perhaps they want it back," he says,
"it might be sacred." "Well, they're most likely
dead," I smile, "their seed
dispersed, in you, in me . . . So it
belongs to the future we are.
The same holds if I got it from
an artist. For art, if paid enough, is generous."
He stares at it so as not to glare
at me, and speaks in heavy tones
about culture. Not wanting anything
to break, I don't dispute
the term, only say that my aim
is to own and emasculate
all gods. He leaves angrily,
walks fearfully
among those types whose taste for violent
amusements scarcely substitutes for violence
and who like neither him nor me.

Must Go On

Rehearsals were dogged by illness, weather,
bad checks, breakdown of lights
and sound, the incompetence
of assistants, the habits of the director.
But the star wanted (needed)
the role, showed up, helped out, set
a standard. Then disaster struck.
As she picked herself up
and staggered among shards
of sets, grid, catwalk, lights, she
hugged to her breast the swaddled
doll from the second act.
Hushed it, cupped
its head, drew round it her vivid
serape, now almost too
convincing because of the dust.
Motivation is never a question but
a need. Not What happened? but rather,
say, Water. A child onstage
is all need. Through ruinous air
she peered for some way out of the village,
the flames. But the ghost
of the leading man (a friendly guerrilla)
came to encourage her and
she delivered something resembling
her lines.

Context

Objects from happier times
do not mock.
May raise a questioning eyebrow
like dogs, who also learned that human art.
Or approach with their leash,
though it's you who slipped it.

Decades proved the inherited ashtray
had no other uses.
The photo in ancient plastic
became someone else.
The inlaid box
that held in reverse sequence
pills, paperclips, stamps, and the sun
evades a stranger's gaze.

Sidekick

After fifty pages I decided
he was a kindred spirit. Would recommend him
to anyone possibly interested, or not.
Some entries I skimmed. The repositioning
of a pre-born calf, the death of the horse –
too alien, rural. Like the priest
he felt for some reason he should admire.
But his walks through the forest, his thoughts on
those walks — I could have had them. Did.
The animadversions on Americans,
who seemed to have landed collectively
on the moon, their ebullient mutual slaughter
and vanity in vacuum — these seemed
only slightly more distanced than mine. The dragon
at the edge of the woods, with its glum humor,
had wandered in from my own work!
The house with its beams and hearth
and hanging pots and age-old plaster
dust was there, but elegized so little
it could have been a condo. Likewise
the philosophers-to-be he had known at school —
I envied, devoured, mentally dropped
the names that on his pages
lay flat and youthful. Eventually
I noticed those he didn't mention. Wondered
if he too feared, more than leaf-rot,
that remark I encountered somewhere in Sartre,
"a speck of boredom in the provinces."

Excursion

Corridors think they're innocent —
provide a service.
To our "lifeless," they say "ecumenical."
Take credit for the efficiencies
behind one door, refuse blame
for the neighboring graft and harassment.
The light that fills them is that of the world,
which neither confirms nor denies.

The one who appears had no trouble
getting past the lobby.
Security cannot now be summoned.
His aims differ from those
of Him whose return the gentiles await, but
there may be areas of overlap.
Executives, consultants,
tech support, counsel, whatever brass is
in residence, even temps and gofers
flee their cubicles and corners
and, gibbering and gasping, crowd
the corridors. Hypertension
manifests, clawing
at ties. Various levels
of women try to take
control of themselves, bring order; see
themselves as if from a distance doing so.
The whole crying mass attempts
to fit through the door of the stairwell. Still

in sight of the elevators,
the one who has come
regards the unmanaging managers and
advances. He may be considering "healing,"
but the word itself has become a wound . . .
Through wildly open doors,
he observes fallen chairs, strewn files,
distraught and strobing monitors

that must all be cleaned up.

Events of Today

A block from here, a weedy path
extends along a slope
too steep, a century ago,
for developers. I haven't taken it
in a while. Walked slowly down
to where it starts, slowly back.
But it's nice — it allowed me
to imagine striding up it
to a grand house somehow blameless
and beloved by everyone, where
there would be wine, good talk,
cigars on the verandah.

Later what, dozing,
I thought a riveter
from an ancient propaganda film
was a woodpecker —
a paragon of its kind, or merely
blessed with a hollow tree.

And that honking
car for a moment sounded
as if it expected
mariachi bands, the smell
of spicy roasting meat, hundreds
of clients and friends and relatives
throwing whatever they throw.

The Central Committee

They asked two questions: *Do you think
you could be happy?* and *Do you think
anyone can?* I hesitated,
thought more about the second, but
in each case cited rules, parameters,
quibbled, ran off into abstraction, felt
ashamed. They remained silent
but without contempt or menace
in their eyes, for they had none,
nor fists nor muscles, only
the rags of a charmless uniform
over bone. Likewise the room around us
had from the start been suited
for only a faded grandeur.
In spite of which I gazed with awe
and still a kind of fondness at the domed,
broken skulls, the strengthless tendons
that had usurped or inherited
the role of muse, and whom
I serve with whatever body and soul remain,
and firmly said that happiness is possible.

And So You Shall

After the museum, my friends napped.
Their daughter cooked — something French, complex,
requiring much care. I sat and read
in the study. The grandson entered.
I'd been told he was brilliant, inexplicably drawn
more to the sciences, but so far
we hadn't talked. I was glad to see
he wasn't holding the usual electronics
I assume are inseparable from children.
He perched on a chair. "What are you reading?"
"Oh, a silly story. I'm ashamed —
your grandpa has so many books
I should be looking through." "Why?"
"Well, your grandpa is wise, so they must be too —
I might learn something." "But you want to read
that book. What's it about?"
"A man who goes back through time."
"Why?" "Some terrible things have happened —
not just in his life but in the world —
and he thinks he can change them."
"I know stories like that. If you stopped
your parents from meeting you wouldn't exist.
Or if you killed them."
"This man wants to kill someone else —
a bad man. A whole series of bad men.
And he does, and the world becomes better,
but it isn't *his* world. He finds that out
when he returns to his own time."
"So the world he made split off." "That's right!"
"Why doesn't he stay there?" —
I found that hard to answer, and didn't.

After a while he asked what I
would do if I went back.
"Well, I don't think I'd kill anyone.
I might. But what I'd really like
is to talk to myself
when I was your age, or a little older.
You're going to ask why . . .
He made some mistakes. I could warn him.
But I guess the rule is that one can't."
"I'm going to be a physicist when I
grow up," he said. "I'll try to build
a time machine. Give me the message."

HR

> *Somebody loves us all.*
> — Bishop

You make yourself nice,
accepting, an idiot
(it isn't hard) to join
the others in Activities
at the long, cleared table (still
smelling of easy food;
now, again, urine). And
the voice that marshals you
to cards or therapy
reminds you of something.
Like all simple things, it's
composite — hysteria,
boredom, the faith of wages, fear
of becoming like you, a
cruel tiny power
beneath the buoyant singsong. It
reminds you of trust
and team-building exercises
at Retreats, then of
preschool through Second
Grade. So you know you belong.

Mimesis

But the kid actually went
and did it. The box from
an appliance had been
sitting around since
the appliance was new; he
brought it up, wiped it,
cut out one side, sat
inside and imitated
the people on their channel.
Patriotic fervor, mockery
of uglies, alerts to threats that
didn't need to be named.
He did the sharp smiles and firm
pouts of the blondes, too,
and some commercials. But he also
did enemies — the near-panic
at illogic, the meaningful head-shakes;
when had he seen these?
He would get such a licking!
He did obvious Blacks, late-night hosts.
It may, reluctantly, have
occurred to them that he wasn't
only imitating television but
cartoons about someone
who, deprived of television, makes one.

For stuff online he didn't need a box.

Entanglement

You crouch in darkness amid melted glass
while spider gangs prowl.
I sit in headphones through an evening sipping
wine Corelli would have recognized.
You lecture cheerfully and understood
to something between broccoli and elves,
while I talk mostly to myself
in a room of hating eyes and hidden knives.
Sometimes in sleep (do you sleep?) you're almost
on the other side of the bed,
and each of us repeats that earliest lesson:
same — different — same and different —
working our way to Same.
But by day, beneath however many suns
(is it night where you are?), the light
from one of us will never reach the other,
may not as yet exist. Yet every
motion of limbs you may only, sublimed
to circuitry, remember,
stirs mine, and any thought
I have reminds you that all thought is strange.
Including this one, that the spectrum
will always remain silent but
an importunate and awkward love would reach you.

Old Mirror

Some loss, along lower edge,
of silver. To be expected: time,
loss is
adventure. Specks — here an insect
secreted or died, there a passing drink
spattered. These do not mar,
are missed if wiped;
reflection is the point, not
what. Rough ovals pass
or annoyingly linger, checking
lines, lipstick, tears, traces
of self. Are not the point;
the point is reflection.

Night in the Zone

Those in the plaza after nightfall look
like dancers waiting for a pause
in the music to end. It doesn't,
but their postures never slacken.
The surrounding ministries, all glass,
proclaim the cause of sleep;
the arching streetlamps seem to long for mist.
Tactfully, unobtrusively,
official shadows move
from one still figure to another.
They tell a shawl her lover waits
beyond those ever-open gates,
a cigarette that his lost — stolen! —
fortune is there; approach
a mound of silent wakeful children,
accompany them out. Now the square
looks more a stage. Two bright
though long-dead stars outface the light,
a dull breeze wanders here and there,
the moon appears mislaid.

One in a trenchcoat, her beauty, even
her exhaustion of another time,
clings to a shadow that remains
to comfort, guard, or spy on those
who linger in the square. She weeps
about warehouses full
of dead, whole latitudes of rape
and torture, the languor of justice,
the impotence of example. The note
resulting on a shadow clipboard may

be "Bitterness." No remark
or physical contact for
her distant possible descendant who,
cross-legged by a lamppost, decries
a fantasy neither bought
nor wanted, the burden placed
by dreams and people and a certain
judgmental atmosphere — he gestures
at the ministerial windows —
on his personal space.

However long and onerous its shift,
a shadow knows it will find
companionship, acceptance by the side
of one who, homeless or a statue, is
a fixture in this place. Who holds
an absurd quill pen, looks off
into the dark as if the darkness spoke.
"Tough night?" he asks as, sighing,
the shadow joins with it, replying,
"Romantics . . ." "I often wonder
what those who follow through the gate
really expect. For that matter,
what those who *don't* go hope for.
The unaffiliated dream is best —
at least, the most suggestive."
Silence. He gazes unoffended towards
the gate, which if it closed
would bring on day and so must never close.
For want of other stimulus, he likes
its sculpted golden vines and iron spikes.

You May Find Yourself

Bumpercars still exist!
In lofty glowing caverns
beneath Helsinki, Montreal,
cities that built down against the cold
or extended the concept Bomb Shelter
to life. Remember the murderous
stalking, the oneness
with power as you pursued
and blocked and smashed another car,
transmuting rage to laughter. There are also
go-karts, for those
whose thing is speed, that solitary sex.

But why not think instead
of horses? Protected, that is

free, on some island, prairie,
or still-grassy corner
of Asia? They rear up, nuzzle, swing
long necks like cranes of muscle. Sniff
at foals, snort. Their eyes lack
the widened whites of panic. They run
for hours, seemingly indifferent
to thirst and dust, because
they can. (Perhaps there's
a testing or mild hierarchy involved.)

And as long as you've gone
full vitalist, imagine lovers.
Love. Your choice
of whom to inhabit, your place and mine
both yours, or an Hôtel Splendide.
The amazing geography.
Another drinker never clearly seen. Or
be brave and posit marriage!
In sleep, a name; even, surprisingly,
yours. A sort of weather,
constant through what becomes
a long morning together.

The rain has its own thoughts
and pursues them at length.
The truck turning into your street
is history, delivering through the rain
only history; one could almost feel sorry.
You've been downstairs, there was nothing;
climbing is difficult, and it's
hard to invent someone
to write. But silence
has its own purposes, and will
reward you for how well you fill
your role.

Role Model

It must have been in Mother's third trimester
that I began to hear talk
about "having something to fall back on."
Retreating as far as I could
in my cramped quarters, I brooded.
"Fall back on" what? Nonbeing? I'd barely left.
And *from* what? One still has, at that point,
some enthusiasm for life; but I gathered
the smugly servile voice meant something else.

The larger question was, Who was talking?
My aunts and uncles were gentle,
much put upon, not "successful."
My parents were arty types; they'd never give me
a rung on or push up the ladder.
It must have been the Spirit of the Age,
one of delis and printshops, not trillionaires.

Nevertheless I came out arguing
with whoever it was. Nothing I had to say
was lucrative, i.e., necessary.
But as I spoke — I went on a long time —
necessity itself, abashed, retreated,
and only what I had to say was left.

The Cicerone

This was the corner. I took out
the photo to confirm. For their own reasons,
the communists then the West had left
the cobblestones, but rooflines were the same,
and the old church tower. The figure
in a white shirt with a righteous bestial snarl,
holding whatever club had come to hand,
must have died decades since, surrounded by grandkids.
Other figures blurred; even the dead
seemed to have hurried into bloody heaps.
The Germans who arrived the next day
were pleased by local vigor but not its disorder.
A Starbucks that had replaced
whatever had replaced the tailor shop
afforded a view unavailable then.

And of course he was there, as always,
a stranger but accepted by the natives
of all these places. Old, respectable,
here doubtless for good reason, pleasant
but unapproachable even to local gangs.
My drink went on his endless tab,
his suit and features merged with shadow,
and he said, as he does everywhere:
"I didn't plan it. I intended
space as the distance crossed in an embrace,
time as the joyful tension needed
to solve a problem, as in art or math.
You can say I was uninformed,
and that it was long ago, though nothing is."

Colonel Bogey

Flat taste of insight
at the end of a real, i.e., hurried
introspection. I always
saw myself as a victim, but didn't
like so many
make a cult out of it (any personality
is a cult). No, I retained
to the end at least
a *physiological* hope, a song in
my heart (that march from
The Bridge on the River Kwai).

Which sounds flattering. But the insight
was that the accomplished victim
works at it, navigates
the turbid inland sea
of psychology, can take it
to court, and never really wants
the enemy to die
for where would heshethey be
without him? While I, far-roaming,
always returned
to hate.

Paintings of Texas Towns

Rod Penner

They are consecrate to Zeno.
For you would have to
cross half that street, and before that
half that, and so on, to reach
the block-long building, bricks still whole,
windows in place, though transparency may
have leached from them. What it was
(which means whose end it served,
for being, here, is profit) is
an easier question than what it is.
Or where the pavement of the street yields
to that before a row of rusted shutters
(which could have been a problem for police
at some point, or lawyers).
Or how long that puddle, defining
a declivity in the dust of
the road, has been there,
or why one bulkhead light
still shines above what may have been a store.
The question doesn't meaningfully
arise, however, where people are.

When Names Drop

There are people I don't meet,
conversations I never have.
I imagine them, however —
specifically the "wisdom of the staircase"
afterwards, cursing myself
for what I should have said! Or the solitary
rehearsal the night before,
psyching myself for battle, so that when
the day comes I'm exhausted,
weary of ego, and retreat to civility,
at best ambiguity,
awakening again myself and here.

At Davos, Heidegger v. Cassirer . . .
We all know who won and who was clearer.

My current interlocutor
represents all six branches
at once of Bloom's "School of Resentment."
He (let's say "he")
displays the elusive eye
and deadly stingers of a jellyfish.
He admits my rhythms are strong, but says
my traditional syntax and narrative,
not to mention that "I,"
are imperialist, male, and oppressive!
I seek a reply,
i.e., a dismissive apothegm,
then tell him he's right, that my strophes are obviously
blackshirted legions trampling him and his kind! Things

degenerate from there. How I yearn
for a lively friendly meeting of elite
equals! As in 1908:
the Douanier Rousseau's birthday party,
himself on a throne hewn from a packing crate,
blissfully drunk, telling Picasso,
"You and I are the greatest painters in the world,
I in the modern style and you in the Egyptian."

Gate of Horn

My best ideas come from the edge
of sleep, where financial projections
are doubted, the medical question
tabled, the report on means and ends
returned for editing; where a corrupt yet timid
republic yields with a sigh to a king, who is
swiftly deposed by a shadowy, place-holder
god, who turns over power to
a khan, maddest of rulers, deeply
wishing the good of all yet
given to laughter and debauchery
in his distant, isolated,
soundproof palace . . . It's he, who fears nothing,
who encourages promulgation
of world-overthrowing, anarcho-critical

ideas that are entirely suppressed or,
if not, sent back for peer review though
peerless, subjected to focus groups
that never quite focus, are
burnt by reactionary forces and gather
dust for decades in the files of

the standing committee.

Gleam

Evil, defeated, and waiting,
some move towards famous fellow-prisoners
whom others shun as far as possible.
The avoiders hope that hair-dye, beard,
no beard, fake documents,
and hard drives long since burnt will save them,
meanwhile mentally assembling
names, dates, locations of money
and arms for the sake of a deal . . .
there's always a deal. That faith
is shared and such plans made
also by those who join the little circles,
though at the center of these, hysterics
hold forth. Hard to tell
what *they* feel, elaborating, sharpening
connections among (bad) capitalists, foreign
powers, cannibal pederasts, mindless
hordes, women, and, always and everywhere,
the people behind them . . . They do it
very well, automatically; perhaps
it calms, defers awareness of
defeat, is itself vengeance; but those
who pray and ask their listeners to pray,
lay hands, say Amen, somehow gradually
lose audience . . . At a
distance, in corners, (good)
executives and owners talk
more quietly, in smaller groups,
unpleasantly silent when someone intrudes,
describing boltholes, their views and defenses,
as if trying to sell them, as if they were there; and
what waits in certain accounts and safes

if they could reach them . . . And mention,
sincerely, formulaically,
families. But when one or another
inveighs, as if by contagion,
against the forces preachers, politicos
and personalities nearby are cursing,
he too loses hearers. Against walls are seated
those who, even if they had
equal status, have
(because they are seated) lost it;
even if they haven't collapsed,
hugging knees, head between them. Even if
they glare into elsewhere, hiss
the rosary of their hates, remember
the good days, beatings, women, money,
one for the other. They are
good soldiers. But even soldiers
may have a mutant thought concerning
what they'd be doing and the enemy feeling
if it were he who sat defeated and waiting.

Drive

Self-driven electric cars controlled
by a continent-wide grid won't make
you passive. Project onto the car:
it enjoys both a rational freedom
(obeying and agreeing) and beauty
(if not, like you, the landscape,
then speed, the wind, being centered in its lane);
precision is beauty. Hands folded, attempt
meditations historically
confined to stuffy studies, while
the foothills and the gentle sweeping curves
progress. By now, wind turbines
along the slopes are bigger simpler trees,
the fields of solar panels complement
the mountains. Kilometer-wide
bridges connect the meadows and forests
on either side of the road; bears, foxes, aurochs
glance down at you, not in the least alarmed.

(I love saying things like this.
They think it's irony, or that modern
degenerate form the put-on;
then realize it isn't, and leave me
consistent and alone,
correct state for a visionary.)

Around the lakes and reservoir
in the higher hills, most houses are
palatial communes, but some are small,
private, hiding (why that?)
among revived Dutch elms. In one,
a woman checks a long-marinated,
slow-baking pseudo-roast, changes,
unnecessarily, her outfit, gazes at
the driveway, gestures inscrutably.

Assignment

A course; the assignment
a modern-classic memoir-novel
about a family. She made the mistake
of asking if we liked it.
Many at once, then each, vehemently,
yes. Tears cited. "I was *there*."
"That was *my* father. And mother."
"Could be any culture." "Beautiful."
"I had to skip, it was so painful."
"I didn't finish," I said, reluctantly
and only when asked. "Why not?"
"I found the father insufferable —
a loud, dismissive egotist.
And for over a hundred pages they simply
accept him, never criticize,
love him . . . then from what I gather
she married someone exactly like him.
No one rebels." Immediate, general,
scornful or flippant protest.
"Rebellion isn't always —"
someone began, more mildly; another:
"Life —" She asked me to go on.
"I'm allergic to novels
about families. Actually, to families.
I wish there was another way
to construct personalities."
"I'm curious what you would say,"
she mused, "if they weren't
characters in a book, but standing here?"

Enemies of the Paranoiac

They were animals of some sort —
assemblages of fangs and palps,
Redonesque, as if flesh were
unserious, interchangeable,
a convenience.
The worse things got, the more genteel
their ironic hypothetical voices —
bored, even; so that
at the end the least flick
of a tentacle would mean
comprehensive pain and shame while,
at last within hearing, they would discuss
future feeding.

With age comes diffuseness. Walks
to build irretrievable strength,
long thoughtless intervals, the young
passing unjudged.
Recognizing in these things
mere eerie contingency —
the last insult, the consummation
of all plots!
The leashed dog who watched
with interest, not growling;
the cat in a second-floor
window, behind a screen,
who said, I could have loved you.

Crasher

The party is for those who have been hurt.
You tour the excellent bar and the long
specialized tables
of fingerfood, wondering if and why
you were invited. Surely [insert memories
a, b, and c] don't compare
with the sufferings of others! . . .
(Proud of yourself for thinking this.) Suddenly
afraid of encountering people
you hurt, you try
to mingle unobtrusively. But beneath
the chandeliers and arching ceilings, scarfing
the delicious salads and sliders, everyone
sticks out. "Haunted" eyes
attain the glow of what they saw. Shoulders
curved against remembered blows
or words frame drinks. You try not
to stare at those with scars or attendants, or
the laughers, but not to stare
is to stare. Music
from various rooms, though the big stage is empty.
Long-dead knee-slapping peasant dances,
severe blues, nearly atonal
solo threnodies, all fervent and discordant and
you wonder if that's the entertainment;
then, actually looking around, you realize
you are.

The Bells

The sense of something having slipped one's mind
was sadder for the old, but familiar
to everyone. Throughout the warm fall day
peasants brought in the harvest, and
the bailiffs of the local nobles
appeared, demanding half. That's a lot,
said the peasants. We'd go hungry,
and why should we give you any?
Well the Count, began one bailiff, owns . . .
but the terms seemed graceless, odd, farfetched,
even to him. How large is his family?
a peasant asked. I'd gladly give them some
of my wheat if they need it, though I can't
see why . . . Uncomfortable, straining
to remember, the bailiff threatened; and men
in hot unwieldy metal did in fact
descend on villages. Those on horseback
seemed naturally vicious, but others wondered
what they were doing and why; where fights
broke out, the peasants' greater numbers told.
In famine districts, castles were seized
or simply entered, granaries opened. In
the towns, people in pointed hats
living terribly cramped in one quarter couldn't
remember why; nor could anyone else,
and gradually they found accommodation.

An old man wondered why his robes,
though finely made, were thick and ostentatious.
He recalled the use of keys and locks, but
not that of golden circles filling
a chest — they were pretty, but signified . . .?
He also felt, hearing a woman sing
in the square where she turned a pig on a spit
for an appreciative crowd, as if life
in some yet unknown way had passed him by,
and went down for his share. He wore
the simplest clothes he could find,
leaving off the mysterious symbol
that everyone noticed everywhere. It occasioned
debate, the tortured man sometimes upon it
pity and disgust. I've always thought,
said a cobbler, that the universe
is divided into active and passive forces.
These aren't halves, however —
it's *quartered*, if you see what I mean.
He too gained a crowd; there was so much to discuss.
Day waned, and from habit
men rang enormous bells in various towers.
People liked the sound — it was solemn but could
seem upbeat — yet wondered what it meant.
They decided that it demarcated time.

Three "I" Poems

1

I've been called on, very politely,
to write something for "ordinary,
unsophisticated" people. No
allusions to "obscure" / "European"
art, "martyred socialists,"
etc. *Subtext* is fine but make the
piece as a whole
"accessible." Funny.
Moving. What's wrong
with that? I'm supposed to
like people, "see their potential," believe
in love. Make it as loving
as a child, or, OK, a
Down syndrome child. As thoughtful
and kind as an abuser between beatings.

2

You didn't see me in the darkness.
I have the knack of not being noticed, or felt
watching. I was watching you.
Saw what you did, saw you leave, and what
you left. Thought of calling
the police or waiting
for the eventual arrival
of what they ideally represent. Thought
in more detail of blackmail —
drawing down, that is, your power, building
mine, till stasis was regained
with only our respective places in it
reversed; meanwhile evading
your attacks . . . but remained in darkness.
Told no one. Why not?
Because I enjoy
too much the potential power of my knowing,
exactly counterbalancing my fear.

3

Things are so confused
now that even
the formerly reliable rising tension
in nightmares is disturbed. The dreams themselves
are no surprise: volcanos erupt —
all over the world, I know, but the one
after me is carbonizing
jungle, terraced farms; the soldiers,
instead of being corrupt and killing us,
are trying to help, leading us (with nothing, some
goats) downhill. But the lava advances —
noise, heat, stench, sometimes becoming
a tsunami chasing one across damp sand.
And all this will pick up where it left off,
I know, but for a moment,
in a room heavy with silica,
a favorite philosopher
gazes across a table, coughs, and reminds me
that the order of ideas is that of things.

Ideal Glass

Hard to say why the phrase so
attracts me. It leads the mind
to unfamiliar territory —
molecules in a fluid, slowing
when cooled but forbidden
by a hundred generations
of glassblowers to crystallize. No;
they retain the chaos
of a liquid but aren't. They
bond, are strong, they
stop — though not entirely:
atoms wriggle, electrons
tunnel. To stop them, to cool
enough for the Ideal
to be reached would take
more time than the universe affords.
Meanwhile, glass is
a "long-range amorphous order" —
you can see
why that would attract me.

Geneva

A delegation is announced;
a position paper issued.
The authorities pledge full and prompt
attention, release copies
to scholars, legal consultants, and
the responsible press. Who praise
its obvious sincerity but condemn
its inordinate length.
Surely the sufferings mentioned,
though regrettable and urgent, don't
belong under one rubric!
The style, with its diffuse,
repetitive sensuality lacks
appeal. It should also be stated
that righting particular wrongs can cause
others. The day comes,
bright and still
as always. The delegation,
greeted by quiet crowds
of supporters, their banners
bearing the emblems of parties formed
for the occasion, the Hoof and Fern,
the Tentacle, waddles
along the Quai du Mont-Blanc, past the Jet d'Eau.
Gossip concerns the struggles required
for cows, whales, pigs on the ramp
to the slaughterhouse, choking
forests, blighted fish and coral to
allow themselves to be represented
by ducks. But the ducks
seem properly solemn; their leader wears
a little sash. They enter the Angleterre,
tomorrow to present their case
to the League of Nations.

Reform

Eventually the "problem of policing"
is dealt with in that city:
tentative, underfunded
programs are put in place
over loud Republican mockery.
But it isn't the wife or a kid
who makes the first call
to the new Mental Help
number — they've had no phone
for a month, as well as no food
for days and no power forever. It's
a neighbor, tired of listening
to the screaming and banging from
in there. Keen, focused,
wearing supposedly calming
green safety vests, the twenty-something
Helpers stand at the termite-eaten
door, identifying themselves, addressing
the person in crisis
by name, saying they'd like
to help. But he has
a gun, which, after a compact speech
invoking a former boss, parole officers,
named cops, the President and members
of other races, he fires through
the door. When the police arrive,
they draw their guns with the grace
of any entity fulfilling
its nature. On her gurney
the girl Helper says, There's a reason
there are more guns than people in
this country, they're the real people . . .

Vieira da Silva

"Le Promeneur Invisible," 1951

Although unborn or very young
when it was built or grew
(too young to know the difference, if there is one),
you know this place. There's a part
of nature that creates
straight lines, flat planes, obsessive tiling.
The levels propagate: you may
encounter color, shadow, even air,
perhaps the locker where you left your things.
The complex mutated into a mall.
You stared and stared, because it promised all
diversion, i.e., happiness;
toys to begin with, if there's
a difference between them and what came later.
Meanwhile the strata multiplied,
providing hidden escalators, while some
hovered like enormous Tarot cards,
still potent though effaced. And gradually
became the coffee table, shelves and walls of
a room, where what is hanging
robs history for timelessness, and the books
already mourn you, though they found you wanting.

Meeting

My torturer is a fundie, his method
sleep-deprivation. Perhaps it seems kind:
exhaustion being its own excuse,
freeing one from cares of the day,
the threat of tomorrow, overestimation
of life and loyalties; and if I talk,
he will reward me with a dateless sleep.
But whether out of machismo, showing
his Jesus-strength, or simply because now
he has a purpose (me), he too
stays awake, doesn't hand me off to others,
and so far has only asked if I
would like to pray with him. Which has
a contrary effect: I tell him,
as politely as one can, thirsty and filthy
and tired, that for me "faith"
is the worst four-letter word.
As always when I say such things,
he smiles and seems to inflate
as if ingesting nutriment. Earlier,
I pointed out he can't meaningfully
or wittily respond, has nothing to say,
knows nothing, would lose strength
replying. Which, I went on,
puts paid to the sentimentalists
(now in his pay or dead) who said
that people like him and people like me
should *listen* to each other: I could only,
hopelessly, instruct him (e.g.,
about history, physics, geology); he would
hear nothing. Now, disjointedly,

I cite extortions, incest, rapes
committed by his type. Say that the error
of my side was from the first to ignore
and despise, not simply hate. We were true
to your lie, but where there's no language
there is only victory or defeat.
The smile persists but he swells more.
Al-salaatu khayrun min al-nawm, I announce;
and before he thinks I'm speaking
in tongues, I tell him
it's what the muezzin cries after dawn,
that prayer is better than sleep.

Infrastructure

1

The poets Godzilla and Kong are
good friends. But one must live,
and each appears in films made for the masses.
Eventually the perverse and limited
minds that rule the industry make them
costars, to the great dismay of both.
Their combat, to begin with,
is as fake as TV wrestling. As cities
shatter beneath their feet, they argue —
their subtleties perceived as howls and grunts —
art. The dispute isn't primarily
one of form. In his lightless den,
infused with poisoned currents, Godzilla loves
the warm (mammalian!) heart voicing its truth.
Sick, meanwhile, of his island with its pointless
gossip and status-antics, Kong dreams
of detachment. Conversing via
Gaia has over the years been pleasant,
but standing toe to toe and fang to fang
heightens words and the scene. Till, tired and
not having heard the command to Cut!,
they stop. The set, the earth
is as ruined as the sea.
Amidst the rubble Godzilla finds
the fragments of an FX tech
who used to slip him drinks, and
breaks down. It's left
to Kong to compose and declaim
over the waste a dry but compelling elegy —
in deference to his friend pounding
his chest once, lightly.

2

The Simoorg also dwells
on an island. But geography is different:
there is no ocean but the World-Ocean.
And on that island stands a tree,
which she on her first takeoff shook
so that it scattered seeds around the world
that became all living things.
She doesn't see that origin as past,
or feel diminished love
towards anything that grows. But geography,
as I said, is simple:
really there are only kings and kingdoms.
And the occasional cumbersome brother
or bastard son who gets exposed on mountains.
The Simoorg hears the cries of one of these
(he cries lustily), flies long
and tirelessly, grips
the handle of his basket in her jaws
(she has the face of the most loyal dog)
and brings him to her Tree. There she teaches him
all the wisdom she knows, which is all wisdom.
But the prince thinks only of revenge and kingdom,
and once he's grown she yields to his pleading, flies
him back. He descends from
his mountain, gathers
an army of the disaffected, slaughters
the favored brother, reigns. Disaffection, however,
remains, unaccountably grows; as his
palace is surrounded he prays
to the Simoorg his mother to return.
There's no response. Unbeknownst to him
(no sailor), the World-Sea has been
replaced by our familiar stormy oceans.

3

One face in the photograph looks
at us; the others
at an unseen speaker, whose remark
has somehow elicited
both (suddenly confident) laughter and
a stiffening of the salute —
the bent left arm, the clenched left fist!
They aren't armed, but look
as if they could be, even expect to be
soon. The building behind them
is not, at the moment, a going concern
(but will again become so, under new
yet essentially the same
management). He alone
looks out, thickset, his expression
watchful and thoughtful. Any number
of planes might strafe, or
cops (still on horseback?) enter
the composition. Did.
His thoughts are there behind the faded photo
and were, and are, as real.
I try to follow them through darkness.
Rising tides, incremental improvement, the Social
Compact were a happy myth,
but time per se is darkness.
There someone snarls that he will never trust
unions, the government, immigrants, minorities,
anyone but his heavily-armed self.
I argue, but another voice advises:
Myth has no memory of myth.

4

The President and I are walking.
I don't know which of us is more embarrassed,
unless of course it's the Secret Service.
History with its cameras
and silly shouted questions stands
at the usual, safe, distorting distance.
So do my followers. I'm warm enough
with a shawl around my robes, but I worry
about the President, older, in his bomber jacket.
I never met, I tell him needlessly,
your predecessor, but stories
where I come from precisely
identify the sort of demon
he was. The current President
smiles vaguely: silence on certain points
is as close as he can come to cleansing sunlight.
We pass a square that looks as if
death happened there. I pray briefly;
he bows his head. Then a structure
from which old voices chant obscenely;
they have claimed so long, I tell him,
that they would die for what they call
freedom that now they equate the two,
and refuse vaccines. For whose timely distribution
my people thank you. He speaks slowly,
judiciously about the battle
for minds. We come to the vacant factories,
the poisoned river and the rusting bridge,
where we discuss his infrastructure plan.
He can of course say little, though what he says
is sincere. Noticing neither
how the bridge ends and always did,
halfway, nor in my eyes
a thwarted lifelong hunger for departure.

Late Valentine

The last emperor of that dynasty
went mad. As barbarian horsemen
trampled his armies in the western waste,
he proclaimed a new palace in
the mountains. A dragon
had shown it to him in a dream.
Whole herds of dragons could disport
on its terraces, bathe in its pools.
Half his surviving peasantry could dine there;
each beam, each fluted tile would be propitious!
The greatest architect of the age,
not even a eunuch, stayed loyal to
the madman. Who confided
that the idea had not come,
as he had told his concubines, from
the dragon of genius, but a barbarian god.
Whose powers were immense though somehow plebeian,
and whose kingdom was distastefully far away.
He wished, this god, to stand
with his consort at some distant time
on a balcony of the new palace,
embrace her, state his deathless love
while enjoying the view of huts and woods and peaks,
and could not be gainsaid. The architect
drew up plans, work even began. But now
the valley is dammed, there isn't even
a ruin, just semi-adequate workers' housing.
I'm sorry, honey . . . he tried.

Legacy

Their names remembered like old phone-numbers,
or vanished, though the face remains,
and the last ambiguous laugh, or request for a loan . . .
Best to regard them as scientists, explorers,
lost somewhere. One discovered
the effect of forty acid trips
in one semester on a mind
that might have rivaled Goethe's. One
who loathed computers when they appeared
became their master, hidden in that fortress.
One researched for ten years with Scholastic rigor
unrequited love, then boringly,
hermetically, theorized women. And, finding
profession, promotion, family, one found me
a vestigial organ, subject to infection, best
removed. But the cases
that keep me up, trying to remember names,
cafés, disputes, are less clear . . .
It's only certain that the fault was mine.

Explorers, certainly, for all of us
"moved." I imagine them
in towns I never visited, every turn
of every street available on screens
but where the later, all-revealing face
never appears, while
the googled bio seems a fantasy . . .
Scientists, too; for they learned
new accents, tastes, ways of accommodating
and dying. In any case
the dullest will bequeath ten thousand facts,
I a few mysteries.

Déjeuner sur l'Herbe

Flanked by a water-feature, shoals
of azaleas and an Italianate row
of cypresses, we set down our baskets.
For a lark, we adopted
the postures and gestures
of Manet's luncheon party.
The costumes were wrong: Sean in bell-bottoms
(the style revived then dead again, but he was
committed), Sharon in shorts not chemise,
myself as usual in cargo pants.
Jane took off all her clothes, sat head in hand;
the resulting erotic charge lent our tableau
conviction. "At least," she said,
"I'm historical — I refer to the Sixties
of the last century, before disillusion."

A billionaire had given us this leisure —
trying, after refusing
to sell vaccines at cost to the Third World,
to improve his image. At least among intellectuals;
intellectuals come cheap. But now a cloud
passed over the sun. Jane put her clothes
back on, and, bagging our plastics,
we proceeded to earn our grants.
Sharon danced the spring. Sean failed
to make a simple tune more interesting.
Jane sketched the water-feature, adding something
extraneous. I wrote a poem,
which, I decided, could have been written
by anyone. I wondered if that mattered;
certainly it wouldn't to our patron.

Skull

I don't belong,
I gather. Where they found me is
too deep. As they keep digging,
they find a rock on which I made
metaphysical markings. These seem not
to go with the size of my brain-case, about which
they make some rude remarks,
though not as vile as those concerning
my family. Or the remaining teeth
with which I had to hold the meat I cut
and are scored by the stone I cut with.

I'm glad when they finally
hold me up; my massive empty orbits
take in a lot of sky. One theorizes re
the jungle. You call this a jungle?
It's pitiful. I try to tell them
I love what they've done with the place, but it's hard in
my state. But perhaps they pick up on it,
for amidst their excited chatter
about papers and awards they mention
"irony" — something about my carvings —
and speculate about my view of things.

They should only know.

Release

After many years a magnetic field,
an atmosphere and seas are laid
and stabilized, soil ground
from rock or coaxed from sand.
Glaciers seeded by the purest snow
descend as far as needed. Rivers
wind over lowlands; lakes reflect
stars still constellationless
and, for the sake of tides,
a clutch of captured moons.
For a while the only residents
eat the sallow grasses and each other,
sparingly, which is also how they breed;
the measured sun their only neighbor.

Then there are houses, lights as well
as stars at night, and someone
whose desklamp is the first to shine
alone and make the hour late.
Who has walked without fear
among the fragile woods and savored
exquisitely a place without the dead.

Erased

Trying to be calm, to create
a relationship with someone
who can't conceive of one,
the victim — who will die
in a moment or a dreadful week —
says, "You don't have to do this."
Why does the psychopath laugh?
Is it because he *wants*
to do this, and finds
the imputation of compulsion
demeaning? Does the compulsion nullify
(so obviously that one has to laugh)
the concept choice?
Are gods involved? Or does nihilism
as lifestyle void the distinction
between choice and compulsion? The killer
can't be relied on
to theorize coherently, and, canceling
future recordings, we invoke
a household watchword, "Just another psychopath."

Among the Elders

A sunbeam from the upper terrace found
and dazzled me; I retreated
towards shadow. Despite the heat
my questioners huddled round a brazier,
at which they stared. They presented
a sad and interesting rhythm
of off-white robes, beards, hair
and clouded eyes. Speaking as usual
as if to vacancy, one said,
"We still don't understand
your thoughts on miracles." I sought
a new way to phrase them, but mostly,
abashed, repeated what I'd said:
"If we believe we know
Who performed a miracle and, even more,
why, does it deserve the name?
Does it really transcend
nature? Or is it merely part
(though implying greater powers
than ours) of the normal ruck
of purposes, another link in the chain?
Truly to worship miracles, we should
begin not end with them,
reject all source or reason, leave them free;
for they are, and alone can free us."

Consternation among the elders,
but with their constant almost ghostly
detachment. "You dismiss
the Shaper and Sharer of all secrets,
the One who comforts me at night," said one,
who as always spoke for all. But in
another's eyes I saw a momentary
glint, as if he had imagined
youth returning, and the strength
and spirit it had borne – returning
suddenly, enduringly, and gratis.
I didn't answer, tried not to smile,
reflecting that my presence, my
existence was itself the sort of thing
I taught. Slowly the light
from the upper story circled the chamber,
bleaching my hair and garment, curving
my back so I could take my place among them.

Line from Eliot

First, the cold friction of expiring sense . . .

Eyes as they dim attempt
the glare of a leader, or
the certainty and calm
of another leader; fail.
Glasses bring screens
and the young bodies horribly
at home in them closer. And
words, but words themselves
seem unreliable, evasive.
Alone, eyes at each moment fear
they show the loss and need they once
contained. Which they won't accept,
because, when they see them,
they must still mock and dismiss them.

Ears in contrast
find peace. When a wind
fiercer than any remembered brings
down leaves in the prime of life,
removing gadgets stills it.
Likewise certain voices. Quarrels,
danger can be outsourced
to eyes, which can close.
That sudden, always somehow surprising
silence is flattery;
important sounds may pierce it, but
they too can be ignored.
An innermost revelation: even you
needn't listen to you.

Baron's Blues

Refusing to retreat
to one wing or suite
of the palace, the Baron
spends what comes in on
repairs. Dry rot, broken
panes are despatched
like intimate foes
in duels, once.
Things extend as far
as cleaning the chandelier
but he buys nothing new. Thirty
places at dinner, the best crystal;
he eats local vegetables alone.
Wears an apron to tackle
corners and cobwebs,
a tux to sit
with one cigarette
and glass as he orates
to blackened portraits
and argues with his books. Feels
faint, sometimes; stumbles
across parquet,
room after room to a heavy
curtain through which,
uncomprehending, he peers
at the crazed marchers.

The Toys

Somewhere in modernity, a New Woman
exits a stagedoor. The bloodstreaked ghostpale
makeup for her role
as ingenue in *Goddess in the Underground*
has yielded to freshness; next season,
if various plots mature, she will be Goddess.
The stalls' and critics' ecstasies
linger. Her silent assistant bears away
several nose-cones
of roses. She will find them vased
at home — save one,
stolen to grace
the assistant's tiny immigrant apartment
and watered by nameless emotions.
A streetlamp limns the actress's better profile.
Droshkies and broughams jingle to the curb,
are displaced (horses clopping
droop-headed off) by a jeep,
MG, and Rolls. A studied gesture
brings glove to dimple, choosing.

Across the street, an aging youth
wearing the Pierrot costume the system
demands of rebels, glares at the suitor cars
with a jealousy that at least is real.
He should be off being a genius
or blogging but in a way
he is at his post. Now fascists pass,
breaking heads and windows, obstructing his view.
(The driver of the jeep calls
HQ, but the time to shoot them
has passed.) The youth is tempted
to join them — let anger out, it's easier
to despise women — but a miraculous,

unmotivated niceness
prevents. He goes off
to mitigate Third World conditions
several blocks away. At times the very white
whites of the eyes in dark
faces in lightless rooms remind him
how he looked at her.

Soon she's the Goddess,
awaiting her car and chauffeur,
head full of film contracts and leading men,
when along the boulevard, narrowly avoiding
bouquets of surveillance cameras, swoops
a new two-person jetpack. It's
a youth she has seen at the edge of the world,
well-dressed enough beneath the helmet.
He invites her for a spin.
I can give you my autograph here, she says,
and Pierrot, imploding, cries
that what he wants is her love – that since he saw her
as the Rebel Girl last year he can see nothing else;
neither ethics nor action nor madness nor pride
helps. How did you get the jetpack?
she asks. He shrugs, sighs.
She lets him down efficiently but gently.
He squares his shoulders, tells himself and her
it must be Art
she has decided to live for. No.

Incident

In the third year, war returned him
to his village. Through a viewport
he saw familiar barns,
houses, the Party office
fall. He was only the forward gunner
but felt as if *he* steered
through walls, pursuing German tanks
that also knocked them down.
He recognized only one
civilian corpse, an old woman. His
column didn't stop
in that village:
they had enough fuel
to advance to the next.

With peace he returned. Rebuilding
was not a priority for
the Center, but neither were the survivors
resettled. He worked.
A third of town was a tangle
of tanks from both armies;
some were cut for scrap.
He was not a reflective man.
Didn't need to be: the years-long
seepage of oil,
high explosives, rust
down a bare slope to a stream
was memory.

The Hutch

No party ever needed
all those stacked saucers, little cups,
the faux-folk yellow-dotted pitcher,
the smaller and larger beveled
bowls, the Deco coffeepot;
we never knew that many people.
Or, by the grey rear wall, the plates
painted with ca. 1900
"spirits" labels — women clothed
in grapes or ascending from bubbles, grinning
to celebrate the victories of men,
their secret triumph being they aren't real.

They live in an attractive,
perpetually clean shadow. The point
of furniture like this, whatever the style
of objects grateful for escape and peace
within, is subtle:
The vulgar put trophies there,
but mostly the idea is elegy
for the idea of effort . . . then, as a quiet
infinite regression
occurs on those shelves, for Time's great wrap party.
Till, gazing through the glass,
I effect another mutation,
seeing them as all the words I'll never use.

Alright

The boys will be out of the house soon.
Tom, daytrading, has covered
his first two years' tuition. Mitch
is doing something I don't understand
with Bitcoin. And Jane,
our youngest, has something going
where girls her age who win can be
real princesses for a day; runners-up
get the unicorn. I couldn't
be prouder . . . Helen always wished
they would play more outside, but I saw
no harm in the ever-expanding,
modular Nautilus, the treadmill that gave them
videos of country lanes, foreign streets,
rap, Bloomberg, whatever they wanted.
But are they socialized enough? she asks. Well,
I observe interactions, and it seems to me
that everyone in their cohort
is more or less on the same wavelength.
Even thugs and bullies, druggies and
self-mutilators (not that we have
too many of those here) are just
a few hormones or synapses,
or, let's be honest, dollars, off,
and know it, and shrug. Our boys
were always quiet — seemed in advance
to have it all figured out.
But they're really affectionate,
and we've always been totally supportive.
So, things are good
at home. Tomorrow we're off to the beach,
dismissing their shared dream about tsunamis.

The Void

Someone had left a book on the arm
of an Adirondack chair facing
the green. No — a book and
a notebook: open, notes in a round,
earnest cursive. And on a picnic table,
something I didn't recognize
at first: a soap-bubble bottle,
open, the circle one blows through
attached to the lid. In this case too
I smiled at an old technology.
In the bough of a tree hung
a balloon — a vivid royal Mylar blue,
perhaps torn. It wasn't high;
someone could have grabbed
the dangling string. I waited
for it to heal itself, reinflate
from a secret canister, detach itself
and, carefully judging altitude
and course, float back to its child;
it didn't. Far away
a dog barked repeatedly,
then from a greater distance
more; perhaps it was saying
that all the wars were over, peace was nigh.

Between the Acts

Between the acts they play cards,
sleep, drink — the stars sparingly,
the rest not, because everyone expects them
to misbehave onstage —
and text. All have networks
whose illnesses, liaisons, deaths, dreams, deals
they keep up on — so predictable
one feels they should have numerical codes,
as should one's own condolences and blessings.
Some dis the production,
but really, what can one say,
for in this realm art has collapsed into life
and critique *is* the play.
A pangolin, career in doubt,
evades the director's eye.
A snake obsessively repeats her line. The sheep
have never quite known what they're doing
but are doing alright; only the crow
gets a note. Everyone seeks
approval from the bear, who scratches his back
on a prop. He ate before the show —
if he hadn't he wouldn't be
so helpful and jolly.

Template

Often in school I disliked
the lack of room for individual
expression in assignments.
Someone comes to visit
(one essay question read).
What is the purpose of the baseball bat
the visitor carries? Is it
to invite you to a friendly game
or brain you? What is
the gender of your visitor [henceforth V]?
The sex? What can the wood
or metal of the bat, the fabric of the clothes
V wears (which may, remember,
be male or female) tell us
about our economic relations
with other countries? How about
the weather? Is it relevant
except as an indicator
of climate change? You may ask the same question
about V's body language and facial expression.
Restricting yourself to these elements,
construct a narrative of your encounter. Be
creative. — This didn't interest me at all,
but the question piqued
the math side of my brain, and I imagined
a template by which one
could determine instantly
the usefulness and/or hostility
of any visitor. Got a C
minus. That was typical. Which is, I suppose,
why no one visits.

Locale

They were working at small tables, on small projects,
but size can be deceptive.
Cool sun and clean breeze
came through the open windows, and it seemed
the day would last until they didn't need it.
No sign of a boss — he wasn't necessary,
if he had ever been.
And they joked and discussed things
quietly, briefly but, I sensed, helpfully

in a language I didn't understand
though it contained mine. I wanted
to beg them for a table and a task;
their looks, pleasant and curious,
implied they would have given me
all needed coaching . . . but I went away.
It is a timeless error to arrive early.

Old Trial

Their drama is austere, stylized
beyond Noh. (They don't see it that way,
emotionally cued as they are to the least gesture.)
In this one an artist —
a playwright, but it's understood
he stands for all artists –
is put on trial in ancient times
for ignoring the real life of the people,
their wisdom, their sufferings,
in favor of abstraction, ambiguity.
The prosecutor's speeches
are fiery and sincere; he is
not caricatured. The sentence would be blindness.

The artist defends himself.
He is never sardonic, dismissive —
often, in fact, he must be told to speak up.
He says the gods do not declare their purposes.
May not even know them, yet direct the great world-theater,
and expect our worship, that is our applause.
That every law which rules mankind
is a script torn up in performance,
and every judge like every king
an actor, yet order is maintained.
And that every word he has written, including
the play in question and this present one,
only imitate, reverently,
the confusion of the gods —
thus setting before the masses an example of piety.

As he speaks, at times singing,
his words are parsed and praised
by a black-clad narrator downstage. Who tells us
that the playwright convinced the court and was freed and
    honored,
later becoming a stern magistrate.

Vergangenheitsbewältigung

Perhaps, in the end, something similar
will happen here . . .
The fathers, disarmed, lose weight
on the poor rations of the first year.
Find socially wholesome work
they hate or throw themselves into
fanatically. Feel surrounded
by less-than-humans, freaks,
and animals they can no longer hunt,
though actually no one comes near them. Meet
in secret, reminisce about rallies,
sing old songs, plot and are
again defeated; breed.

The second generation, changed,
accuses. But this is America
and there's a crazy religiosity,
still, about them . . .
Minorities, not so minority now,
rebuilding the cities laugh
at the son of a magapreacher,
who is always hanging around, wanting
to help. "*I'm* responsible
for him / it / everything!" he weeps.
His significant other cries "You're not!"
but eventually finds him wanting —
the way a German girl I knew
in the '70s said that German girls
despised "Softis."

The Draw

The poets of my youth, who defined me
as more than a weird non-baseball kid,
play cards in heaven. They aren't
in someone's home. (No one's ever home
here. You crash when and where
you need — some sofa.) It's a suite, super-classy,
in a sort of ultra-Vegas.
Playboy bunnies and Chippendale guys
bring beer and smokes and clean ashtrays.
(Drinks tend to make one
too lucid and sardonic, so one sticks
to beer.) A disco ball projects
the galaxies, or the scudding leaves and petals
of formalist poems. When a bio
or Collected Letters is published, a player
may suffer slight arthritis or
a rash, till he makes a clean breast
(the phrase intrigued me in my early teens) of
his evil weekends, beatings, adulteries,
vacuity — which everyone
knows anyway. They vie with
each other. ("I *hated* visiting Pound!
but you had to.") As for work:
Kerouac attends every mass.
Ginsberg is sure there's some mistake
("Why am I trapped in *this* bardo?"), shows no one
what he's writing. Yevtushenko
wants to do something fresh and whole;
"The political situation finally
permits," says Rexroth. Ferlinghetti, more kindly,
advises that since heaven is
eternity, all that a timely mind
can get of it is an image.

E. Bishop holds an inside straight.

The Perks

It was a long sentence, not
entirely fair, but I've stopped
insisting I was innocent.
Now I relate to much younger people,
young enough to value "experience,"
and see me as one, and surreptitiously
seek wisdom. They're still there,
beneath the hard-wired disappointment
(no assets but youth, no prospect but loss),
and stop to talk. The girls
radiate . . . like a solar corona
above the mistrust and whatever dysphoria;
I don't look at them. Speak

in parables. There was a dead Northern poet
or capitalist (the difference fades
on the Other Side). He had expected
a cold white church and cousins,
ex-wives in florid outfits,
colleagues feeling nothing much.
Then the earth, leached of metaphor,
or fire, which, to insensate flesh
represents all the crap that *didn't* happen.
Instead it was someplace southerly:
dust, whitewashed walls, and professional
mourners following, howling, breast-beating, swaddled
in black, over the top. He thought
of climbing out of the carriage, grabbing one,
demanding "Who hired you?" but didn't . . .
he found he liked them.

They drop a quarter in my cup.

Firebird

When you defeat them — as you'll have to,
at the cost of more blood
than you can imagine, even when pitying
your current designated objects
of pity — remember:
you must, with your new, stern,
disgusted lack of sentiment, punish
their fragments if they ever use
the image of the phoenix. They don't
deserve it. They are never reborn
but always the same. Their growth
is rot. Their thought
is sleep. They have
no single molecule or chemical
in common with the Bird
who will rise from the ashes
they are — rise, with the insouciance
of an animal, a victor,
reason.

The Coin

Methods of execution there
are baroque and public.
On the eve, the high priest of the province,
whose hair is as white as his robes, his mien
a god's, traditionally visits
the cells. It is in his remit
to pardon one of the condemned. Mad with terror,
they plead, scream, grovel, throw shit
he mostly dodges; it appears he won't counsel
this batch about the interworld,
its opportunities for more fortunate
incarnations. One among them, however,
sane though very pale,
bows and says nothing. "Why are you here?" asks the priest.
"I was the greatest thief in the province,"
the doomed man says without pride.
His story requested, he says, "My parents were poor,
but I reached third rank in the examinations.
I dabbled, however, in forbidden texts
and magic, questioned the graciousness
of the gods, disputed the system of
rebirth, and was expelled.
Starving, I went to the city
where I fell in with a gang,
which soon, having wit and few scruples,
I led. We accumulated riches
I intended to send, in large part, to my parents;
but when I was betrayed and taken,
your lot and the prefect stole it all."
"And what have you thought here?" asks the priest.
"I perceive and worship a great mountain,
with the gods, of course, at the top,
then the emperor, you, etc. Neither

the peasants I grew up among
nor my former associates are crushed by it;
rather, we live in the valley
and must climb on our knees the lowest slope."
"And do you repudiate
your earlier heresies?" "Of course," says the prisoner,
his cracked lips smiling. The priest
absolves him of his crimes with a gesture

that the prisoner, leaving the prison,
reflects upon. Was it that
of tossing a coin to a beggar?
Or to a market woman?
Hungry, he lurks by the market, filches
an onion. His home is too far off,
and if he went he would find no one there.
He can't return to the city:
new gangs reject old kings,
and the life, if truth be told, had sickened him,
and the place was always poor.
Wandering, he comes to a cemetery.
A procession has just left; he is drawn
by the smell of new-turned earth.
A man beside his wife,
who had died the year before. Their little virtues
are inscribed on little streamers;
the flowers are bright, the incense has stopped.
He finds himself weeping. Then the high priest
who had pardoned him is somehow there,
saying, "Always a thief."

Solidarity

Not loud, quiet, and not the quietness
of passive-aggression; what's intolerable
is the engrained assumption
of privilege: that what he says is
important, that he is.
That anyone should care
how in his dreams he too is pursued
by cops, or the private guards
of some plutocrat, or
gangsters identical to police
(some smaller countries lead
the world in this respect). How he's accused
of offenses that aren't,
or wouldn't be if they weren't his,
and beaten till he wakes; how he lives
in wasted time. And through
their shouting they attempt to make
the distinction between his dreams and
their lives. But in his eyes
and sunken posture they perceive
(with contempt and a sort of relief as well as
compassion) that he's simply mad,
and lift him gently, call someplace
for help. Thus solidarity is achieved.

One Thing or Another

One thing or another prevents you
from going out, and you tell yourself
it doesn't matter: the air
is fresh enough in here, the trees
along the street are busy and don't care
if you look at them; why should you feel
this irrational guilt?
(Well, exercise — but really . . .)
Clubs and rock concerts were never your thing;
if you went you would look both silly
and eerie. The museums are closed
or half-closed, letting people in
selectively, testing for appreciation.
And people — one can't just drop in on them . . .
There's dust
on a sideboard, a chair is out of alignment –
you fix these. Perhaps where the street
goes out of sight it's all ruins, but
you're still being given power, water, light;
as if you were a trillionaire
with your own zipcode, in a sort
of modern castle, exclusively
bonding with other castles and fearing
only barbarians, who are never adequately
identified, though doing so
is the sole function of language.

Darlin' you just sorta

Back then they had bodies, hopes, and student debt.

She was it, as far as he was concerned.

When she met the other guy, everyone knew.

Decades later he returned to that scruffy town.

Time had fucked them both up. She said she was sorry.

He said at some length that it was OK.

Now just student debt.

The Prophet Drinks

1630

All that I have laboriously made known
will again be hidden — buried in the soil
of the mind, which is always muddy,
however parched the wider earth.
There it will rest, while our admirable barmaid
fills your mugs, evades your hands,
and reminds herself not to be stupid
when that young sergeant laughs a certain way,
and you, whom I address because
it amuses you, and me, think nothing at all.
Outside, the stragglers of a great battle
continually pass, but have
no coin or voice or gut for wine or beer;
your local priest or pastor senses them
and closes the church door.
On a branch above the stink of the hanged
a crow has built his nest,
disconsolate, although he has fed well,
at the paltry straw from the last harvest.
But the seed sprouts in the mind
and will grow to a great speaking tree,
perhaps when your bastards tend it, or when
the casks are empty and there's none to hear.

Ballo in Maschera

It is made clear that if the masks
are removed without permission, consequences
will be dire: an unpleasant mechanism
is contained in each. Some of the feistier
or more desperate ask Why these
masks, anyway? They only show
inane young faces. And the brighter
among them figure out: but they don't change.
Then tuxedos and gowns are fitted
and cummerbunds and heels. Some, quite unaccustomed,
must be taught how to wear them; all, swiftly and fiercely,
how to move. (It's evident, however,
that, resentment aside, many like what they see
in the many mirrors, through their eyeslits.)
They stand about, still badly-postured, gorgeous.
After these sticks, the carrot: they're told
that if they perform well, *youth* will return,
with all its quirks and lusts.
Among which later thoughts and memories
will have to settle; where is up to them.
In any case, by evening's end,
the face and mask will match. The atmosphere changes.
Some know how to dance, as distinct
from solitary jerks and wriggles; these
are urged to teach the others very quickly.
The less poisonous artists, scholars somewhat
immune to jargon are given protocols
for wit, feminists for flirting;
professionals are told to be themselves.
They have half an hour to practice,
and after twenty minutes someone laughs.
Then they're all ushered into the ballroom. Gape
like rubes at the chandeliers.
Music, marble pillars, decorative
guards with gleaming bayonets and buttons.
Great doors, which open,
and someone disturbingly familiar enters.

Glyph

We asked the alien to show us something
from its culture. Like everything
beyond mere math, this took forever
to get across, but the alien was
as always inhumanly patient.
On its side of the screen, it inscribed
a figure like an extended comb
or inverted centipede, with one prong
or hair extending upward from the center.
An unattractive as well as inscrutable
symbol, I thought, but an ethnologist
on the human team became excited.
"You find this all over the world," she cried.
"From Australia to the Sahara to Arizona.
It dates back forty thousand years."
Some muttering began about ancient contact,
which seemed unlikely. The days, I thought,
go by, with their deaths and hunting
and other feeding and mating, and then
one day *I'm* there, *I* do this,
and then the days march on.

Namatianus

Understandably, few works of art
can be securely dated to this era.
Some tunes remain, diffused.
An apocalyptic mural
effaced by graffiti. A possibly sculpted
mound, mid-desert.
One might wish for an equivalent
of Namatianus's
shortsighted and meanspirited
poem of his perilous voyage to his surviving
estate in Gaul, or Ausonius's
nostalgic, lovely "The Moselle."
But there are only notebooks
retrieved by chance
(one tends to avoid the term "miracle"), and
the final brittle pages of a typescript,
quite different in tone from the rest.

Something I Said

It's worse
than remarks that ended
job interviews, dates, jobs, relationships.
(She sat there crying or enraged,
and since I'm nice I apologized
for months or the duration.)
I turn from whoever it is,
staring and pale, and myself. There are depths
of self and wit I'd rather weren't.
But a waitress here with hors-d'oeuvres,
though impeccably trained, has dropped them,
the tray aghast in midair.
A general has almost spilled his drink.
A celebrity ages. Noted lobbyists
and cokeheads, always in motion, stop.
Hidden children whisper. From the terrace
a wolfhound enters, steals some human food,
and gazes up with doubtful sympathy.
(In the distance, workers
erecting a tent for the raffle grin,
but they're from the past, some old novel.)
Across the salon our host and hostess
stand motionless, still gracious.
I should bottle it, I think,
by which I mean keep silent but connote
researching, mastering this skill,
inventing time travel and returning
to stymie history with well-placed words.

Friends

A genius director, menaced
in his neofascist homeland,
accepts an invitation to New York.
His thing is improv. Even the music
("graffiti on the fourth wall," he calls it)
is improvised. A loft is made up
as a comfortable apartment — kitchen, shower.
The accomplished advanced student actors
he has chosen are told to regard
the circulating shadowy small audience
at the rear as the unconcerned witnesses
their city is rich in. "You must act,"
he says in his impenetrable accent,
"for a week. You have no roles but aren't you.
Must decide in the course of things who you want to be
and are." An Asian girl who heretofore
had shown no sign of gender dystrophy
is a man from the getgo. He holds forth
on the *misères* of women in a way
that gradually reveals his vanity. A trans youth
interrupts, proclaims male virtues, however
latent and hard to evoke. Unsure
if they're being ironic, a pair who
offstage are not lovers mount a fierce married quarrel
about chores; then cook, which renews it.
The cast eats in silence. The poet
(who rather awkwardly declares himself)
engages the couple about their jobs,
improbably lucrative, hilariously insecure.

The comic turn works but risks stasis. The trans
inquires mildly of the husband
when he'll afford a yacht like Bezos's
with its own service yacht. The Asian girl,
now uneasily female again with a caricatured
accent, refers to "Celestial Ships"
and warns them not to sail the South China Sea.
The poet, worried, soliloquizes
about how, when institutions functioned,
one could valorize the individual, the rebel,
but now, in his own work at least,
he finds himself dreaming of bureaus.
The third day, however, the wife breaks. She had tried
to hold on to the music, which at least came
(when it came) from outside, but it
had failed her. Now she slams
the door of the microwave, curses, and
goes looking for the genius, who is nowhere.

Echo

I've *already used* the title I want:
"Guitar, French Horn." Which looks
both pretentious and naked mid-stanza.

The apparent lack of a sonata
for that combo makes me happy (I could write one)
and sad (I don't know how).

A small, close room. The distance.
Confidences. Regret.
Interpretation. The given.

Vision in Georgetown

They seem distressed that I'm more interested
in them than in their holy building
(in my notes a word like "church," but it isn't one).
Politely, as ever — all emotion swaddled
in ritual packaging. Could never form
a mob: though they face me, smiling,
they'd obviously rather turn away;
from each other too. Know about videos
(at least I think that's the word),
but when I don't create one they nod:
the dreamtime never left, is always here,
will never come. More and more pour out
of the little houses — once, we know,
the homes of the poor, then the rich,
now of vines and flowers cupping cherished glass;
the old brick variously patched,
the walls held up by centuries of scrap,
and they themselves now small enough again
to fit. The building is as tall,
they point out, as a hundred of them, and
significantly windowless. They have kept nature
from reclaiming it. Signage gone
except for a beloved lightning-bolt,
the sole (this also meaningful) door all rust.
Gently I ask them what they think is in there;
their voices always gentle, they reply
"Power." Just before
the estuary claims the street, a sort
of knotted pampas grass obstructs the view,
the remains of yachts entangled in it.
We think one is a Predator Sunseeker.

Low Orbit

In time zones consecrate to deepest sleep,
walls fall one night.
Dreams, which normally and however cruelly
play among them, flee.
Without those sequestering walls
or the deceptive focus dreams provide,
you perceive neighbors.
If you're fortunate, the nearest country
is familiar, ruled by compromises and
evading laws you know, mutually
smuggling, with much-toured public shrines
and secret ones known to Intelligence;
and as you lie inert, your unaccustomed
eye overflies her, perhaps wondering
whether she too is a lucky country.
But if you're alone, you sense
you too are being surveyed;
someone whose dog, at least, you know by sight
may have a job with its own satellite.
His landscape is flat, except for one temple
where daily horrid offerings occur.
He must think you're an adoring worshiper;
otherwise wouldn't he raise
an army and find sleep impossible . . .
But currently the nations seem at peace
and open to inspection. Even those
that are mostly swamp. Where refugees fled ruins,
then over years as long as generations

drift back to them. Where every act
of love involves a faceless paramour
who vanishes at dawn. Where dusky forests
invade the approaching hours, and contain beasts,
which become hunters . . . while, beyond
mountains that you and distant neighbors raise
to exclude them, savage territories
yearn and plot to get to you for want
of a true target. Yet even they
repose tonight beneath a sky
that strikes you as innocent, however dark.
Imagine fleets of satellites up there,
secure somehow from space junk, with this data.
Perhaps if day did not rebuild the walls
they would defy their operators; share.

Witsec

Someplace you can easily blend in.
But I've become so obedient,
quiet, grateful for attention,
and was always, if truth be told
(which it is, I've told it) colorless,
I could blend in anyplace.
Anywhere people walk with canes,
the halt, the blind, haters of cold,
sufferers. (I don't discuss the cane, the lasting
fruit of a brief misunderstanding.
I miss the one my late associates bought me.)
The agents — the usual three,
a pleasant girl, one harsh one silent guy —
show pictures of a bungalow
twelve limping blocks from a crowded beach.
It will do. An office
where I shall uncreatively keep accounts.
Local amenities one could, I suppose,
develop a taste for. I nod
and nod. I nod at all the rules.
They want me to sign, for the last time, my real name.
Are surprised when I say
I want my former boss to show me around
the house, his genuinely evil
woman to choose the suits I will wear
to work, his chief enforcer,
crushing every impulse, to swing my hammock.

Empty Parable

Once he returned, D. told me this joke
as a way of explaining why he attempted
suicide there. For some reason
two guys have to cross, without skis,
an icy snowy waste. They lace up their boots,
shoulder packs. The first day
the first guy slips on a snow-covered rock,
goes sprawling. Rises painfully,
catches up with his friend and says, "Damned hidden rocks!"
They proceed. Night falls. Put up the tent.
Wind howls. One reads Marx, the other a thriller.
The second day, the black mountains ever nearer:
reindeer. Their smoking breath, earthen smell,
oddly musical grunts, that look
which might be undespairing. At least
they're not being illegally slaughtered, thinks one
of the guys. The herders, little fellows
in layers of vivid faded wool,
do not turn, except maybe once, with
antipathy. Light snow. That evening
the Northern Lights appear, like
a gigantic living thing if life had no
concern for consistent form. A possibly
illusory smell of ozone freshens
the cold wind. On the third day they reach
where they're going, mysterious in the joke,
at the foot of the black mountains.
Second guy says, "Yup."

The Towel

The lover sits unnoticed in a corner.
He has taken the form of a print on the wall,
a light green jacket hung from the back of a chair.
The composition of the print,
the fact that the jacket might slip
are that delightful painful tension
a lover feels. So is
the sound of West Side traffic through
the closed window (it's autumn). He wishes
that noise weren't here but, behind
the half-open door of her bathroom, she
ignores it. Towels herself dry.
(The towel is two-thirds as long as herself.)
In the mirror checks for lines — there are none.
A new hair dryer has a pleasant warmth
and roar, as if furnaces had cubs.
Her hair is compliant. Though her thoughts
are elsewhere, the hair frames
her face like one. The robe
on the back of the bathroom door is also green.
In a moment the lover will be there;
but for now, though glad, she has only begun
to prepare. Steps into the room, half-lowers
the blind, hangs up the jacket,
and is at this moment
the way she might exist in an old man's mind.

For the Centenary of H. S. Mauberley

In the South Seas, he picks up a bug.
Thereafter, though never entirely well,
he can't die. Other symptoms: time
is screwed up (the wars merge). He finds
he can no longer express himself
in sharp-hewn stanzas packed with Greek,
Middle French, other lore
that no one understands any more,
or pretends to, or is even willing to wait
for footnotes. Years in sanitaria, full
(to spite him!) of incurable ghost Jews,
who show him their poetry. He
discharges himself, is on hand
for the *épuration* (Brasillach with
his last breath mourns "great red fascism,"
which strikes M as prescient). Gets
in touch with Pound, and is one of the flacks
sitting round in '67 when
the Master sort of blames himself
and Ginsberg sort of forgives him. But M,
not stupid, sees that for the masses
the only analogue for him and his style
is Zelig. Mr. Nixon, of the famed
"steam yacht" (destroyed in the Blitz), has died
and left him advice: "Go into advertising."
M does. His commercials allude
to every jewel and layer of Pop; he's
hot. But sometimes culture warriors
unearth his background and he has to change
his name or firm. Alas, he moans
one night in his flat, Art goes
through cycles, the ironic, the sentimental;
you have to cut your soul to the pattern.
A chronic drop from the kitchen faucet
lands in an unwashed pot. As it fills,
the sound becomes deeper and somehow doubled.
One could write that, he thinks, but it would be
only another sort of vanity.

Dig

I'm so far back that I'm scarcely
historical any more. Wide-hatted, white
with sunblock (that technology doesn't change),
kneeling she draws the latest GPR
across the dust to find some part of me.
The words I read and those I wrote are gone,
but I insanely, non-negotiably
believe they're not, that we will talk.
She weeps at the lack of progress, the ambiguous
walls, the flies, the depths of broken glass,
the waste. But now she strokes me
with a brush, and photographs and raises — what?
One can't evoke the rock one will become.

Years later, clean, alone in the sort of bed
I insist on for the future, she dreams
we're face to face and asks disappointing,
quotidian questions. (She's so young;
they would all strike us as young.) I explain
what she already knows better than I,
adding some hopefully useful private grief.
She's curious, though handling the word with tongs,
about the *religions* that roiled my time;
the category in her soft mouth seems
to include nearly everything.
My faith, I tell her, was a narrow drain
through which the filthy cosmos trickled out.

No Problem

The nation of humanities-
type intellectuals institutes
a space program. There's dissent —
the money would be better spent
on their numerous orphans, preserving
illuminated manuscripts — but, well,
the stars, you know . . . We'll reduce
the first three astronauts chosen, the Commander,
Mission Specialist, and Aphorist
to numbers (1 through 3), which is how
they often feel. They are not the gung-ho
well-adjusted military athletes
of richer countries. Training almost kills them.
Liftoff is worse. Reality has the weight
of seven gravities, thinks 3. True learning-experiences
are deadly. 1 gets in touch
with Ground Control so often that he sounds
needy. 2 hisses a song
of imagined loves beside abandoned highways.
The man in the moon quickly fades but remains
in the mind. (The Chinese, 2 reminds himself,
see a rabbit.) The far side
has fewer features on which to project.
"It's the back of a skull," says 2.
"The truth is the whole," quotes 3 tonelessly;
"the desired object, then what lies behind."
"This is not the place," barks 1, "to go
all Sophocles. ('Call no man lucky unless he's dead.')"
"But that wasn't the line," 2 objects. "It's
'Call no man lucky till he has passed
the borders of this life secure from pain.' The Greeks
were always so wordy." 3's finger
hovers beside
an ill-placed switch. Which, if he pulled it,
would void all air from the capsule.
He doesn't, however, fearing this
would mean an even greater loneliness.

Group

One folding chair in the circle, facing
the same empty center, is filled
by someone different, not so much in dress
as in his or her relationship
to silence: easier.
It may be a bearish man;
an elder, seldom motherly; a girl
who somehow weds officialdom and kindness;
an intent, colorless being. In whom
a tear exists that is never shed:
the grail. One who has taken refuge
in hatred looks at that figure, thinks
I will make you live the way I live
but fails to act, till even boredom fades.
One who has sheltered in silence yearns
to hear that person say what can't be said,
and see it dance or grovel in the center.
And one who can only talk
and talk about the unbearable talks
when called on; what's different
is not the fact of speech but that it ends.

Brood X

They fall on their backs and can't get up.
With the end of a twig I righted one.
It crawled into the grass, possibly flew,
ineptly, hitting something, as they do,
and fell on its back.

Among the dead on the terrace,
one had that fungus
which eats their butts. It resembles concrete.
Also this week, on a science site,
two micro-mushrooms on a living ant.

Forget the sound. You get used to sirens,
planes to and from Reagan National,
news. I've long planned
on my deathbed to curse, also, nature . . .
hope I remember.

Figures in a Room

A guy, not someone we knew but someone
like us, had hurt her.
Psychological abuse.
I imagine us standing, we may not have been.
Determined not to cry, she gave
details and cursed horribly and her curses
involved all males.
R. was there — I think I've captured his horse face,
more pinched the more upset. And my then-girlfriend,
who alone interacted with her
at each stage, and touched her. She's hard to draw.
And S., attenuated, nervous,
whom I remember saying
later, "This is the end of it,"
by which he meant the hopes of that hopeful era.
I thought he was being, as always, rhetorical.

Dramatic but directionless lighting.
Four figures standing around a fifth,
who is enraged but somewhat bowed. Heavy shading.
When de Kooning was old, his assistants put canvas
before him and brushes in
his hand and he painted marvelously —
red quasi-organic forcefields, curvaceous
pink forms outlined in blue, though he couldn't talk.
It would be harder in poetry.
The drawing, which doesn't exist, represents
the poem, which barely does. They avoid each other.

It was one of those buildings near Oakland, later torn down.

High End

He wanted a mosaic floor,
combining obsessive patterns
with anonymous gods and nudes more "real"
(less flat and blocky) than their Roman forebears.
No one had the skill. He paid
some obedient artists to learn the skill.
Then shelves, built into twelve of the longest walls.
Not much of a reader beyond electronics,
he knew what sort of staging impresses
in videos; a professor chose the books.
He also knew that one has to avoid
gold toilets, etc. Then the grounds, the topiary,
the water feature . . .

An interviewer asked how
(this was after the divorce) his personality
was reflected in the house. He could have said
but didn't that since childhood
he had hated walls, however filled
with art, or floors with rugs, that *could* be bare;
rooms that admitted someone else might live there.

That was after his return from space.
His unadmitted fear
throughout was the most memorable
part of the trip. The crew of the space station
smelled chemical, were snowed, cowed,
gushy, showily aloof:
all calculable types.
They tried to impress him with unimportant science.
He enjoyed snapping Coke from midair.

Before They Dropped Salads

You receive a letter. When did that
last happen? (When the post office
they're trying so hard to privatize worked.)
Creased, handwritten
in pencil on lined paper, many pages and
misspellings. You received one like this
years back, but that was recommending Jesus.
Here there are only wounds the system, not
identified as such, keeps open:
the bad pay, no breaks, no job.
One kid's condition, bills.
Two stops in one night, an earlier beatdown,
cop breaking a taillight then ticketing the broken
taillight. Illness. Artless,
whatever grey words come to hand, the only
(unconscious, effective) image a styrofoam
bowl from McDonalds the writer uses
again and again, washing carefully.
Not asking for money, or anything.

You scan and file the pages and respond.
Since you aren't asking for money,
I can only assume you heard of me somehow,
and thought I could write about you, and that that
might help. But you must understand:
I'm a poet, and no one reads poetry
except those who already sympathize
as much as I and are as [substitute something
for "impotent"] as I. You'd do better
to contact a novelist [insert names].
But remember: minorities disapprove
when someone not in a given minority
writes fiction, however sympathetic, about it.

I mention this because you haven't
specified your [race]. — You go on
three more lines, trying to inject
human warmth, then print and sign (that may
be worth something, someday), and fold.
Take out a twenty, hesitate, add another,

then realize there's no return address.

Sermon

I thought at first it was a play,
and wondered who would enjoy
such stasis and pretension.
Those hieratic robes and tone,
an actor who could carry neither off
and took a thousand words to say
Escape is both impossible and a sin.

Absurd, I thought, from a mere warden.
Prisons are waste and pain, not sacred.
Yet to that audience, which filled all space
including what I'd thought was mine . . .
Their worship turned to cheering when,
repeatedly, he invoked freedom,
a thing that died when it became a word.

Grasp

Immune to its charms, ignorant of its names,
I drive into the countryside.
Odors of vegetables and animals.
Hay-fever, chaperone of intellect.
I bear in a cardboard box the relics
of the deceased, suggesting only innocence:
a past, that is, not canceled promise.
The house is as I expect, expecting little,
in need of paint to hide its other needs.
And, knocking, I must remember whether
son, daughter, or whoever is in the box,
for that can influence my reception.
Which will inevitably be bad,
though at first I'm offered a chair and awful coffee
and gaze at pious slogans, framed or carved,
I privately decode, my look approving.
Try to grasp, I urge, that I didn't know him
or her. I'm not the police. I come
long after the police, who were and would be kinder;
it's we around this desperately polished
table who are the cold case now.
She meant to be good, quit drugs, help people,
he to be rich, successful, male —
successful in any case, a star, a patriot!
These toys, that scrap of diary, this key
to a long-emptied safe deposit box
reveal if properly interpreted
their good intentions. The city
was cruel, but with a cruelty you wanted . . .
At which the beating comes. I'm prepared,
faith in non-violence never questioned;
and when, exhausted, he, they stop,
I see in them through my remaining
eye that agonizing choice of troubles,
whether to dispose of me or learn.

Line from Paul Engle

The sun has been definitively
repealed for the day:
thick rain. But the parade
begins on time, undeterred.
The music has a cracked demotic air
with pleasing bursts of atonality.
The majorettes discover irony
in each slurred step and twirl,
the greater weight of cap and braid,
the slippery baton;
the wind is cold across their thighs,
the smile becomes a grin.
The flags droop heavily against their poles;
seem more the idea of a flag
as a flag is, supposedly, an idea;
the colors of the curbside bunting run.
A platoon of undoubted heroes marches
as the band plays, more or less
in step. It's the idea
of synchrony, of discipline, that matters,
though less and less as rain increases,
and irony infects the ranks,
and an unaccustomed pity
for undersized and sneezing comrades.
"'I have heard those marching in the dark go singing'":
a soldier quotes a forgotten poem.
"It isn't dark." "We'll still be marching
when it is. Unless flags dissolve
and banners fall like tarps on our heads
and missiles like fireworks fail
from damp, and our new spirit spreads
over the neighborhoods." "It isn't you
who are saying this," cautions another.
"It's that adumbral figure on the corner
who, madly cheering, has replaced the crowd."

Cardinal or Oriole

He met people — largely thanks
to his sociable wife. Early on,
those people had kids. A child is
a blender. Toys, towels, a variety
of substances, the earlier selves
of the parents, and the child itself
go into that blender and what comes out
is creamier. Later, he observed, grandparents
think they would like to be
that stuff, but it is circumscribed
in their houses. Meanwhile titles, things on walls,
food, where they ate it, and price tags, which
are never entirely removed, told him
over the years what he needed to know
and his wife filled him in on details.

They talked. He talked. When they talked
he tried to marvel at the stuff of life,
children, real estate, doctors, and always,
circularly, the regime.
Remembered that he lived in paradise,
as far above the poor as billionaires
were above him and the talkers. Generally
kept silent, as husbands do
among the sensitive classes.
When he talked, he compressed
as in a late-night talk-show his alien
interests to something humorous;
prided himself on being mostly viewed
as nice; once, when pathos seemed called for,
told how his father, dying, had become a birdwatcher.

Old Song

I keep expecting the culture
will resurrect and spin it
on that only slightly less than cosmic jukebox.
I don't remember the band, the words,
just one crazed interval —
paired megaliths on a flaming alien shore.
But if it played, all parties
would still be on, me dancing, flailing,
hair would return, every hair on my arms
(to speak only of them) would stand up,
and I would be willingly absorbed
by the irresistible firm —
no need for the current hostile takeover.

Late June

Almost too pathetic to be a symbol,
a last cicada husk
clings to the underside of a leaf
on a branch that has been trying all spring
to reach our window. I hope the adult form,
wherever it went, mated,
escaped the monstrous birds,
and contributed its full quota
of song. There must be, across the universe,
any number of species
that see themselves as tragic, but
at most bring to the faces
(if any) of the others
a rueful smile.

The Restaurant at the End of the Universe

"Time" is a useful word
in poems. People know what you mean,
and you seem to know what you mean
but at the same time to mean
something more — as if you have an overview.
Then you can mock it, ignore it,
sound like you're letting them in
on mysteries, which are what they want.
Not billable hours,
three minutes estimated reading time,
How long have I got.

The Beautiful Losses

Nothing guarantees the success
of a new faith more than a pious king
though he calls himself by the antique name
of president, and has at his command
only swords, pikes, and crossbows,
not the legendary engines
that now fill royal dreams.
His realm like all the rest is a narrow strip
between swamp and desert,
which are the green and dun on his coat of arms.
One rare cool week
he proceeds across the land with his court and army.
In the center of the procession
ride priests in wagons. These are women,
and people neither simply men nor women
who are barred from farming and inheritance
but sacred. With the king rides
his counselor, an intellectual,
who frowns at the view from left to right
with what he hopes is an ancient attitude.
"Are you sure he's good?" asks the king.
"He was rigorously examined," says the counselor,
"as were his neighbors." "And he knows
he won't be given land? Only
coin?" "He firmly said, and I believe him,
that your approval is his best reward."
They arrive where they're going,
a raked and dusty square, once a parking lot.
The chosen upper peasant stands in the center,
his tenants behind him,
his frightened wife and children at a distance.
The army camps in the hills.
The king's guard invests the scene, arrows
notched. Courtiers stand about chatting,
or sit on handy folding stools.
Intimidatingly yet kindly,

the priests surround the wife and kids
and ask about their lives. Are they ever beaten?
Is she ever forced? Is he considerate?
An acolyte wonders, If a wife were
as evil as her husband would she not
say everything was fine? But her abbess,
making a holy gesture, nods at the king,
who approaches the farmer but veers off
to ask the tenants questions similar
to those just posed to the family.
Their tearful, strong encomia compete.
The king clasps his subject
and says, "You are a person.
Not a goat, born to be milked and eaten.
Not a horse, recalled from oblivion,
uncomplaining though weary, to serve.
You know that I am more than you
only because I have power
to help and protect you. And that
you are not more than these your servants,
who also help and protect.
That women are sacred and equal, and to
be loved as if they were all my daughters.
That if people whose skin is of different colors
were ever to reappear, they would be friends.
I know all this about you
because people I trust have found you worthy
of trust. And so —"
The counselor steps forth and hands
a leather purse to the farmer. The king
goes on; his voice is strong and carries,
though tremulous with feeling:
"Stamped from the precious substances
of the former world, this wealth will recall —
unnecessarily — our trust in you
as you exact our few requirements:

meat and grain to feed
my soldiery and household,
who are also all your friends and sworn to your service."
Here the voice breaks, and the king leans
his brow against his subject's. All
the square, the assembled villagers, the priests
and courtiers weep. Unheard
by any but the farmer,
the king vouchsafes his hope that the virtuous
dead of the former world
will bless them both and bring back snow and power.
The counselor, a man who fails
to notice little and who, as the wisest
of the ancients advise, says less,
nods at the priests and, more discreetly,
the new publican;
who says, as he was told the rite demands,
"You have my vote, Mister President."
After feasting,
the square is cleared, the royal party leaves,
except for a detachment
of soldiers to be quartered in
what may become a town.
Hand in hand with his wife, the farmer returns
to his house. They wave away flies;
tomorrow she must wash
his and the children's flimsy tunics.
He is not, in fact, a monster
of greed. Will buy more land and men,
tax cautiously. Had little trouble
answering the probing questions
of the priests; only follows
openings where they occur, thinks seldom
of himself or anything. One may doubt
that someday, from that acedia, change will come.

Safe House

She makes the mistake of asking how I'm feeling,
and, typically, instead of taking it
as the blandest social sigh, evading engagement,
I say that, apart from basic, correctly-pronounced
angst, I seldom notice what I'm feeling:
it doesn't help. But she, as fearless, capable,
and beautiful as a movie FBI girl,
smiles and asks in that case what I'm thinking.
A worse mistake. About my work, I tell her;
I would have liked to know, like other poets,
the names and quirks of plants and birds,
myths, peat deposits, far-flung lands
where whites are few and mostly drunk. And bring
together mismatched nouns with brazen
adjectives like drugs in the bloodstream, thereby
breeding cute chimeras. Instead
I have to pick at abstract scabs,
avoiding prose and mere psychology,
and watch the pus of history ooze out,
and do this without liking people much.

Across the room her antitype and colleague,
fat, male, and surly, isn't, I think, snoring;
it's how he breathes. They are, however,
as one in dedication to my welfare,
or so I trust because I have to trust.
The room enthralls me. Why this beige, that white?
Impersonality is an illusion; all
décor is choices, and whoever chose
this way to avoid the personal was like me.

The recessed lighting suits, I announce,
the lady agent, as the almost-shadow
by the laundry-room her comrade. The pink
glass fluted vase, the flaring pine-cone hanging
lamp pay homage to a social-democratic
style, and universal values,
and better times. There are even books
on the shelves: all mysteries, no doubt,
but so was every book I ever loved;
and if this eulogy is my last work,
I hope she'll mention it in her debriefing.

They tense before I even hear
the chant, the somewhat unruly march.
Hands hover beside guns, which are, I quote,
the language of history; they tell me to shut up.
But my internal manifesto
grows louder as the lamps are doused
and filthy torchlight mars the walls
and, ordered to a corner, I sit and wait.
What is the human? Why should one look
behind, around, before, above,
but not with hatred into hating eyes?
Where reason is unwanted, reason,
talk, deny and disrespect
the evil more than the death they seek.
Why should I not replace them?

The Fortunate

Eventually the gods notice
they represent nothing. This bothers them,
the only way gods can be bothered: mildly.
They form commissions, aping,
in this as in all other efforts, humans.
Meetings devolve into grandstanding,
arias, fistfights; some members don't come back
from lunch. At length a somewhat responsible
Steering Committee decides to consult
expert humans. They'll be brought
up and out to the corner of the multiverse
where gods have lived since Epicurus placed
them there; and once they (the humans)
have given what help they can, they'll be returned
to whatever time and place and fate
they left, remembering nothing,
paid only in visions.

The old man is pleased to find himself,
not young, but hale, not needing oxygen
or pills; and, almost more importantly,
remade into an image of himself
he can tolerate (and which, on better days,
away from mirrors, he is).
I've been stylized, he thinks.
The gods don't introduce themselves by name.
Names were initially as understood
as in a childless village, then gave way
to allegorical meanings everyone
found boring. New abstractions
moved in, were grudgingly accepted; now
for them too names have fallen out of use.
One of the latter, blonde,
motherly or vaguely therapeutic
(a MILF, the old man thinks) is there to greet him
(the Steering Committee couldn't get it together).

"You're taking this extremely well," she says.
— "Well, all my life I hoped that aliens
would land, or to encounter people
from the future . . . This is similar, though
less satisfying, if you'll forgive my saying so." —
"I can see that," she smiles. "But consider:
an alien or futurian wouldn't need
your help, most likely, and we do."
She explains at length. They break
for lunch, in a place like the Colombe d'Or
in Vence, with vistas much more Bonnardesque.
Gods also there (primarily to drink)
pay him no more attention than other consultants
at other tables with the same goddess.
With whom he then, not tired at all,
strolls somewhere like the garden at The Cloisters,
which strikes him as beyond ironic.

"I think I see the problem," he says.
"*Meaning* is centralized, like God.
Like modern selves, for that matter. I mean,
if we pray at all, it isn't specific
requests to specialists." The idea of swallows
spirals in the sky. She seems to expect
his next thought, which is, "Like Nature, too . . ."
— "With the big capital N," the goddess nods.
"I know her. She's a bitch, but a friend.
She feels herself superior to us
because you still invoke her." — "But only"
(the old man is catching on) "in a manner of speaking.
Your friend has no *control*. It's all blind processes."
At which a god from another table,
the worse for wear, invites himself to theirs
and thrusts his broken veins at the consultant.
"I hate you smelly insects.

I mean that literally. You smell
of life. You shouldn't be allowed here." —
"I never asked to be," says the old man
bravely. "Or to live, for that matter." —
"We can solve our own problems!" the god yells.
"But we haven't," says the goddess; waves
her (long, smooth-looking) hand; he vanishes.
— "I'm amazed you can do that." — "It saves time," she shrugs.
"He'll return the favor." — "You know,
I would have called him Ares … He may have
a point. Why don't you just forget us?
Forge a new destiny. Explore . . ."
She somewhat sadly shakes her head. "We too
have something like mass media, your overmind,
and are very well informed if we want to be." —
 "Please tell me," begs the human, "is there anyone . . ."
For several minutes she fills him in,

which leaves him both depressed and hopeful.
"Or," he mutters, "you could help."
— She frowns. — "Attempt to reconnect.
Help us." A notebook appears; she makes
a check. "I guess that's not original."
She smiles noncommittally; says, deeply, "Thank you";
their hands meet. Then, all business, she
informs him he can stay as long as he wants,
go home when he's ready; and is gone. A city
rises around him. The museums
contain the originals of works of art,
the coals that fade in us, as Shelley said.
The bars are crowded but unwelcoming. There's
a red-light district, but the goddesses
wear jeweled Minoan robes. "Aren't you hot in that dress?"
he asks. And in a voice like molten gold
she says, "I'm hot no matter what I'm wearing."

View of San Francisco from the Hills

Three from Berkeley, thirtyish.
Two were without (or hopefully between)
women; one lived at the Y.
It was the era after the left but before
the right. In New York the subways
were greenish-brown, tattooed with the rage
of the lower classes, not perceived as such.
Here day was glorious. Earth had trickled
downslope from the path we climbed; we had heard
a deer. Of the others, one was tall, one short.
Of myself I'll say only
I was not a prime specimen.
The short one spoke: "We aren't friends, exactly.
To use a term that becomes more prevalent
with what it names, the depressed
hang out together, for want of better
company or a felt right to it.
(Too little research has been done on this.)
All that we have in common are doubtful finances
and the fact, remarkable in context,
of not being drunks or druggies." Here he lit
my and his cigarettes. "He"
(he nodded at our friend) "leaves his awful
room at the Y, collects via wit
and scattered erudition straight acquaintances
he isn't attracted to; he finds them relaxing.
I do my little jobs
on either side of the white collar, keep
the pickup that drove us here obsessively
in shape; there may be family
money, guilt-money, behind me
but I don't show or speak of it. You,
fatter than I, suffered
more than I on the climb, but notice how
I complimented you, and how firmly,
saying you can really *move*. Such
moments, which I look for,
are my equivalent of social skills."

The tall one meanwhile gazed across the Bay
at the still-new Bank of America
brick, the Transamerica spike, Philip Johnson's
white armoire a-building, the "Corporate Goddesses"
not yet on its mansard. "They will come for me,"
he sighed. Perhaps a ghostly
cheer from long-closed Alcatraz
greeted an aircraft carrier bound for somewhere.
"In buildings like those," he said,
"a new world is being made
with even less room for the likes of us
or any poor. Southeast of them,
in a neighborhood where I've found
as much love as I need, I have sensed
Death planning (the effect is rather Poe-like)
a party beyond hepatitis,
streets full of hearses instead of floats.
But that won't concern you," (this to me)
"who still, as you once let on,
imagine a girl still wearing
the peasant fashions of ten years ago,
undefensive, not rich but whose apartment
has a view of bridge or bay
and who would for some reason let you in . . .
You must accept
she no longer exists, and that power
(including that of males) is making sure
she won't return."
                    And the short one, who often
abridged, I remember,
our friend's more caustic flights,
agreed the cost of living in the City
was insane. Described stopping
for a cappuccino in North Beach; the price
he mentioned seemed incredible
and would now. But the tall one
(I don't recall their names), who sounded
milder as he grew crazier, overrode:

"It doesn't concern me either, really.
This month I've been reading, in Greek,
the so-called Pseudo-Dionysius,
sixth century. He was the first to say
that evil is a lack. That everything
yearns within its capacities
for the Good, which is itself
a yearning, and in the end we'll all
be turned around and go there. I will go there."

Incapable of visions
of the future but unsurprised by them
(I always assumed, and was proud to grasp
new levels of, the worst), I ignored
the religious stuff, if in fact he said it;
if he did, he would have apologized later.
Gazed at the docks, sun glinting
on the stupid vertical streets, fog lifting
(it returns, late afternoons, like a big duvet),
and saw, not felt, how beautiful they were.
Whatever fantasy I'd allowed myself
in this bad period had involved
the City; now I thought
I wouldn't be able to afford them.
Only the latent violence
of the carrier lightened
the absolute, depressive realism; it gave me
an idea; those days I was always having
stillborn ideas. Yet there seemed
an odd transcendence to the scene; perhaps
it knew it was becoming memory.
I talked a lot with those guys
but don't remember anything I said.
Ideas, probably, which they found
as boring as their own, an available
time-killer. Things improved for me
in a year or two, to the point that I
no longer deserved the holy name of loser.

Acknowledgements

"Total," "Piety" in *The Rail*.

"On Culture," "Must Go On" in *The Crank*.

"The Central Committee" in *Dissonance*.

"Enemies of the Paranoiac," "Crasher," "The Bells" in *Survision* (Ireland).

"Why Not" in *Poetry Wivenhoe* (UK).

"Gate of Horn," "The Thermos" in *Flights of the Dragonfly*.

"Brood X" in *Black Poppy Review*.

"Self-Starter," "Something I Said" in *Artvilla*.

"Glyph," "Namatianus," "Something I Said" in *Cerasus Literary Journal* (UK).

"*Vergangenheitsbewältigung*," "Solidarity," "The Toys," "For the Centenary of H. S. Mauberley," "No Problem" in *Danse Macabre*.

"Sermon" in *Literary Heist*

"Legacy," "Grasp" in *Bindweed* (UK).

"Group" in *Rock Paper Poem*.

"Witsec" in *Change Seven*.

"The Perks" in *ZiN Daily* (Croatia).

"The Towel," "Friends" in *Ariel Chart* (Australia).

"Dig" in *Barnstorm*.

"Call" in *Live Nude Poems*.

"One Thing or Another," "The Prophet Drinks" in *Locust Review*.

"The Cicerone" in *New Croton Review*.

"Swivel" in *Cathexis Northwest*.

About the Author

Frederick Pollack is the author of two book-length narrative poems, *The Adventure* (Story Line Press, 1986; reissued April 2022 by Red Hen Press) and *Happiness* (Story Line Press, 1998), and two collections, *A Poverty of Words* (Prolific Press, 2015) and *Landscape with Mutant* (Smokestack Books, UK, 2018). In print, Pollack's work has appeared in *Hudson Review, Salmagundi, Poetry Salzburg Review, Manhattan Review, Skidrow Penthouse, Main Street Rag, Miramar, Chicago Quarterly Review, The Fish Anthology* (Ireland), *Poetry Quarterly Review, Magma* (UK), *Neon* (UK), *Orbis* (UK), *Armarolla, December*, and elsewhere. Online, his poems have appeared in *Big Bridge, Diagram, BlazeVox, Mudlark, Occupoetry, Faircloth Review, Triggerfish, Big Pond Rumours* (Canada), *Misfit, OffCourse* and elsewhere.

Printed in the USA
CPSIA information can be obtained
at www.ICGtesting.com
BVHW052110040823
668232BV00022B/185

9 781737 621959